TH

Lo

IMMIGRANT

THE
Local
IMMIGRANT
The story of a Third Culture kid
who found his way home

Jonty Tan

 **Marshall Cavendish**
Editions

Published in 2022 by Marshall Cavendish Editions
An imprint of Marshall Cavendish International

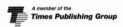
A member of the
Times Publishing Group

Other Marshall Cavendish Offices:
Marshall Cavendish Corporation, 800 Westchester Ave, Suite N-641, Rye Brook,
NY 10573, USA • Marshall Cavendish International (Thailand) Co Ltd, 253 Asoke,
16th Floor, Sukhumvit 21 Road, Klongtoey Nua, Wattana, Bangkok 10110, Thailand
• Marshall Cavendish (Malaysia) Sdn Bhd, Times Subang, Lot 46, Subang Hi-Tech
Industrial Park, Batu Tiga, 40000 Shah Alam, Selangor Darul Ehsan, Malaysia

Marshall Cavendish is a registered trademark of Times Publishing Limited

National Library Board, Singapore Cataloguing-in-Publication Data

Name(s): Tan, Jonty.
Title: The local immigrant : the story of a Third Culture kid who found
his way home / Jonty Tan.
Description: [Singapore] : Marshall Cavendish Editions, 2022.
Identifier(s): ISBN 978-981-5009-82-8 (paperback)
Subject(s): LCSH: Tan, Jonty. | Singapore--Social life and customs. |
Group identity--Singapore.
Classification: DDC 305.80095957--dc23

Printed in Singapore

For Milo and Aspen
May home be where your heart is

CONTENTS

Foreword

As the head of an international school in Singapore, I interview dozens of prospective teachers each year about their chosen career, passion for teaching and desire to come live in an island-nation so often far away from home.

One of my favourite questions in these interviews is: "How does being (insert nationality) inform your identity? In what ways are you quintessentially (insert nationality) and in what ways are you not?"

When I ask this question, there is often a lengthy pause and a response such as, "Wow, I've never been asked that before." Or, "I have to think about that a bit."

I love the question because it tends to unpeel a few layers of the onion and let me know more about the values, perspectives and cultural core of the candidate. I also learn so much about the world and national identity. Many applicants identify with more than one home culture, which adds nuance to their reflection.

Jonty Tan's *The Local Immigrant* presents a compelling and lovingly portrayed response to my question. How do we identify more strongly with some parts of our identity than others? How do early childhood experiences impact us? What role does food have on cultural and personal identity?

In detailing his experiences and reflections of leaving Singapore as a young child, growing up in Britain and returning to Singapore as an adult, I felt like I was reading well-written letters from an old friend sharing new discoveries as he explored culture, identity and self.

One of the book's strengths is that it makes us think about our own formative experiences. I found myself reflecting back to a visit to my childhood home outside Washington, D.C., with my wife a decade ago. My heart pumped a bit faster as we approached Hesketh Street and I saw the thick ivy vines my older brother used to descend from the second story to sneak out to meet the ice cream truck just before dinner time.

The current homeowners saw the two of us standing on the sidewalk, a bit starstruck, and came out to say hello. When learning I had lived there decades ago, they invited us in. It was exhilarating to walk through the house and backyard again. The memories came flooding back: the basement wash basin in the laundry room where I, aged 8, accidentally stapled my chest by pointing the staple gun the wrong way; the stump in the backyard we used for third base in neighborhood baseball games; and the upstairs bedroom where my mom shared that she and my dad were getting divorced.

Childhood memories, connected to place, pack a punch.

Throughout *The Local Immigrant*, Jonty Tan's deep humanity and constant curiosity shine through. In conversations with strangers, reflections on parenting, explorations of Peranakan heritage food, insights into British schooling and adventures into Singapore's Botanical Garden and other island treasures, he leans in, observes and notices the small things.

It's the same kind of approach I've seen him take to his role as a music teacher at our school. Mr. Tan is known as one of those teachers particularly gifted at developing relationships with students because he cares so much about them as people. His hallmark sensitivity makes them feel seen, heard and valued. And his passion for music, learning and discovery inspires students to make connections every day that ultimately enrich their lives.

At the end of his book, the author reminds us of Aristotle's words that self-knowledge is the beginning of wisdom. *The Local Immigrant* is Jonty Tan's walk down that road. How fortunate that we can be fellow travellers on the journey.

Dr. Mark Wenzel
Singapore
December 2021

Chapter 1

Back to Where it All Began

Singapore's highly efficient underground train network, called the MRT (Mass Rapid Transit), is the main vein of the Singaporean body. Trains run on time—all the time—and while they can be packed full with commuters, their cleanliness, air-conditioning and lightly-coloured interiors make it comfortable to travel on, even at peak points of the day. But as I got off the train at Ang Mo Kio station that morning, it was quiet. The Coronavirus global pandemic had caused strict regulations to be put into place that had hugely reduced the crowds and silenced the remaining few commuters with guidelines to not talk to avoid spreading airborne moisture and germs. Singaporeans tend to be fairly quiet on public transport anyway—usually attached to their phones, faces illuminated by their screens—but these guidelines made the silence mandatory. The quiet of the morning amplified the physical feeling of anticipation—a knot that was not quite an ache, not quite butterflies—in the area between my heart and stomach. Any higher, it would force my heart to beat harder and faster in excitement; any lower, and I'd have a deeper, uncomfortable feeling that would be closer to nervousness.

However, this feeling of anticipation was not uncomfortable—it was welcomed.

I walked slowly while my eyes tried to take everything in. The normal, everyday sights of a suburban neighbourhood in Singapore became a canvas to study. I began paying attention to every brush stroke, every shade of every colour, every layer, every person. The wearing of surgical masks had been made mandatory and so I looked into the eyes of the people I passed. I wasn't looking for anything in particular, but I wanted to *see*. I had been to Ang Mo Kio a few weeks earlier, to find a Singtel store to set up my mobile phone. My mission now was to connect with the neighbourhood, to see how it felt to be there. In Japan, the practice of *shinrin-yoku* ("forest bathing") is becoming increasingly popular. Its participants would connect with nature through the senses—sight, smell, touch, taste and sound. For me, this trip to Ang Mo Kio was akin to this practice. I wanted to see if I could learn anything about myself by being immersed in the environment. It may not have been a forest, but to me, it was a form of therapy that I had been waiting many years to experience.

* * *

I was born in 1984 to a Peranakan father and Teochew mother. I had an older sister, Charmaine, who, despite still struggling to grow hair on her head, would soon turn three. I understand from my parents that I was keen to get out, keen to live life outside of the womb, and I arrived before the gynaecologist could change out of his wellington boots. I'm not sure why he would have worn wellingtons in Singapore, but this is the story I have been told. I was brought home to Ang Mo Kio, to an HDB apartment owned by my parents. We didn't live there for long—we moved to the outskirts of London, England before I turned two, but this was my first home, my first neighbourhood, my first community.

Soon after we arrived in the UK, my younger sister, Amanda, was born, completing our family. We must have been a very interesting family to the people at the little church we attended on Sundays. My mother was a high-flyer, working in London in the financial markets—the only woman on the dealing room floor, holding her own in a male-dominated environment. She would describe the banter that flew across the room, but I'm sure she gave us the family-friendly versions. I remember her talking about crazy amounts of money—hundreds of thousands of pounds that she'd lose or make in this fast-paced environment. She recounted to me an evening when she came home after a uniquely bad day and described the financial losses—I was scared at the amount, until she explained to me that it wasn't our family's money! In contrast to my mother's work, my father was a university student, studying for a masters in Arts Management with the dream of one day running a theatre or concert hall. He had studied for his bachelors in the UK as well, and was a talented pianist. He took us around his university campus, Coombehurst House of Kingston University, one afternoon—it had the biggest rhododendron bush I had ever seen.

We had a live-in helper, Lita. She was a kind Filipina with a soft smile, who joined us to take care of me when I was born and travelled with us to England, remaining with us until I was six. A helper, sometimes also referred to as a domestic worker, is quite literally someone who helps with everything you might need in the house, from laundry to cooking, cleaning to taking the kids to school. While helpers in Singapore were and are commonplace, they were unheard of in London and I wondered what people thought of our unique family set up. My parents treated Lita differently to how most employers would have treated their helper. She would join us at the table for meals and she would come with us on outings, as part of the family, rather than as an employee. With my mother's longer working hours and my father's studies, Lita was a parent to me. She moved to Canada after working for my family. We lost touch with her over the years and I still think of her often, even now.

Following his graduation, my father fortunately landed a great job at an independent girls' school in Surrey. He had gone for an interview for the role of piano teacher, and came out with the Head of Music role instead. My mother continued to work in the city and my sisters and I were enrolled in local state schools. As a family, we got into the rhythm of British life with the help of my paternal grandparents. For some reason I struggled to settle into my first school. As a teacher now, I often look back on my childhood and wonder what teachers could have done to support me better as a student, or what it was in my life that caused my trickier behaviours. I have since concluded that Lita's departure was a huge upheaval in my six-year-old life, as well as some harsh and probably unreasonable grandparenting, which is probably worth a whole chapter in itself. My parents were encouraged by my state school to find somewhere else for me to complete my primary education and they decided to place me in the independent school system, which offered more attention through smaller class sizes, and extensive sport, which would help my more active mind and body. I completed my schooling in the independent sector and gained an education that many would see as quintessentially English and privileged. Even some of my English friends, who were educated in the state system, would comment that I was "more British than them".

When I was 12 years old we became British citizens. I don't remember much about the process, other than my parents buying a seven-seater car with a personalised number plate to celebrate. That car was a lot of fun and it took us on family holidays around Europe. The Singaporean Government doesn't allow dual nationality and so we had to renounce our Singapore citizenship and so I became fully British... well, my passport became fully British.

I gained a music scholarship to my senior school—a prestigious independent school for boys in the home county of Surrey. I remember my audition day. I carried my cello in one hand and my bow in the other. Music sheets were tucked under my arm and I stepped into what felt like an enormous concert hall, onto the stage. The chairs in the auditorium were olive green and there were three adjudicators. I don't remember which piece I played or how I felt, but I am grateful that I had that opportunity. I mainly enjoyed school, although I wasn't particularly studious. I loved sport and I enjoyed my music, but academics escaped me. I finished with 13 GCSEs and three-and-a-half A Levels, but I often think I would learn so much more if I went back to school now, as an adult, embracing the opportunities that were presented to me with much more enthusiasm.

The school was fairly multicultural. With a Caucasian majority, there were a good number of students from different countries—India, Pakistan, Iran. There were fewer Orientals—I seem to remember a couple of Japanese students and then me. My heritage was always difficult to explain. I would often be labelled as Chinese—but it was a label I could never own. "I'm Singaporean," I'd say. Most of the students thought Singapore was in China. I very rarely experienced racism in a hateful or prejudiced manner, but I experienced an awful lot of ignorance. People assumed I was Chinese and that my parents probably owned a take-away shop that sold Chinese food and chips. There was an expectation that I was supposed to be good at maths and that I must have known some sort of martial art. Occasionally, when someone had heard of Singapore and knew it as an independent nation, I would get excited and tell them "I'm actually Peranakan." They had no idea what I meant. But nor did I, really. I have since learned that this is a tension often felt by Peranakans, who would use the Malay phrase, "orang Cina, bukan Cina", which translated as "a not-Chinese Chinese person". What I knew of being Peranakan was that we had certain heritage dishes that my grandma would cook and that we have some sort of western blood, probably Portuguese. I guess it helped me to feel like I belonged—having some European DNA.

I never felt like I fitted in the UK. I mean, I loved being there and I had some good friends, but there was always a level of discomfort in my own skin. In certain circles I felt confident, in others, I felt invisible. My school taught me how to be confident, perhaps a little arrogant, as it was a high-flying school, much to the envy of our rival schools and their students. But at school, I never really felt like I could be confident, and so when I was in more comfortable settings like home, or with family friends, the confidence and arrogance I was taught at school could be more openly expressed. My family didn't like the arrogance and I was unaware of it. It made life very difficult. Like a country in conflict, I felt I was hosting residents that didn't belong. In one place, I was taught to be confident and bold, but didn't feel confident or bold; and in another place I was confident and bold, but it wasn't welcome. Eventually I put my discomfort and misplacement down to being an individual. My generation was taught to embrace individuality and so, that must have been it, right? As far as I was concerned, everyone felt a little disjointed, but that was what individuality was all about.

My teenage years were a huge struggle. I succumbed to British culture, and going clubbing at the weekends and drinking too much was a fairly normal occurrence. My mother somehow managed to get me a job in a shoe shop on the local high street and so I enjoyed spending my money on nice clothes, going out with friends and having beers. My parents and I fought a lot. As I got older and stronger, I became more rebellious and more frustrated. Their expectations for me were very different to what I was achieving, and while this was all out of genuine love and care (rather than reputation and face), at the time I felt like it was unfair, restrictive and limiting. Between the ages of 16 and

18, I became more and more distant from my parents as I tried to find my fit. Their culture was different to the one I was living and I needed to find where I belonged in this juxtaposition of values and style. I understand this is very common amongst first-generation immigrant kids. When I left for university at 19, I felt like freedom from my parents was well overdue and my first two years were fairly wild. Throughout that time, I had no doubt my parents loved and supported me. I just needed to work out who I was and who I wanted to become. I needed to understand in which camp I would pitch my tent and which landscape I preferred and why.

It was on meeting a now-great friend called Owen, while I was at university in Norwich, when things changed. He managed to persuade me to go to his church one Sunday morning. Having grown up in a church environment, it was fairly familiar—a cross-section of generations, friendly faces and older folk with an unhealthy enjoyment of quiche. The experience of church itself was wonderful and my subsequent devotion to God is a story for another time (although I guess strands of it will be intertwined in this book), but the pastor of this church made a huge difference in my life and a significant one when it comes to my journey of reconnecting with my Asian roots.

Pastor Tom Rawls was a dynamic leader. An American by birth who had grown up in Australia, he had spent 12 years in Thailand as a missionary, where he was completely immersed in Asian culture. He spoke Thai like a local, he adopted Buddhist values and he loved the local people. Somehow he had ended up in the sleepy city of Norwich in the east of England and his church, intentionally or not, had some very strong Asian cultural features. Honour. Serving one another. Respect. These are all features that a Brit might say are present in British culture, but in Asia these things are present at a different level of operation and intensity. I connected with these cultural values of the church very quickly. I didn't realise at the time that they were already intrinsic to me: after all, I had spent the previous five years suppressing them, hiding them and ignoring them. But as part of the church, they were repackaged with a new label and so I was happy to embrace them.

Pastor Tom treated me like his son. He fed me like his son, loved me like his son and also disciplined me like his son. His style of discipline was more Asian than British. His words were sharp and the tone was sharper. I had matured and grown up a little since childhood as even when I disagreed with him, I honoured, listened and took on board what he had to say. I am grateful for his direction and discipline and I developed resilience and strength of character during that time, gained clear and wholesome direction and I felt that north was reset on my moral compass. More than anything I gained a real sense of purpose that I don't think I had beforehand. I will forever be grateful to him for those years under his leadership.

* * *

I was 29 years old—husband to a beautiful English girl called Millie and father to our rather chubby one-year-old son, Milo. Even my grandma, who usually wants to feed everyone until that moment just before you explode, was concerned that Milo was overfed. We had saved our money for months, buying and cooking only cheap rice and frozen chicken in order to put aside enough to be able to afford a holiday in Singapore. My parents had gone out to work in Singapore as expats and were blessed with enough space for us to be able to stay in their apartment and so we decided that, seeing as a return ticket was the same price regardless of how long we were away, we would have a long, five week holiday. I hadn't been back for six years—the last time had been with my parents, before Millie and I had even met, but I was keen to show her my home country and even more keen to bring my son to where I was born.

I have always valued my heritage, even in giving my kids Chinese names—not that I could write them in Mandarin, or even say them correctly—but knowing my heritage was important and I wanted to make sure my kids didn't forget their roots. Our happy little boy loved his first experience on a plane, which was helped immensely by the Singapore Airlines staff who doted on him. They even sat him on an empty food cart and pushed him up and down the aisles, making him chuckle and warming the hearts of the other passengers. We were grateful to the airline staff for paying him so much attention and I felt super proud of my smiley little boy.

We spent time with family and in trying to do all of the touristy things as we were unsure whether we would return— the Singapore Zoo, Sentosa, East Coast Park, Pulau Ubin. We took in the modernity of the Marina Bay area and we hiked the MacRitchie trail. We thought it would be a once in a lifetime, or at most, a once in a decade sort of trip. Millie and I had an unofficial rule that we wouldn't return to a holiday destination as there was so much more of the world to see, and I guess this was in our mind with regards to Singapore, too.

About two weeks into the holiday I realised that something in me felt different. I couldn't put my finger on what it was, or what had caused it, but I felt more "me". I still find it hard to describe the feeling, but it was like a weight off my chest, like I could breathe more easily, like I could let my guard down a little and just be myself. What was it that caused this feeling? I'm not sure. Perhaps it was the culture, or the weather, or the food, or the heritage. Perhaps it was all of it. Millie, a rural born-and-bred girl, fell in love with the modern metropolis, and at the end of our holiday, started to search the internet for jobs. But I wasn't ready to leave England. It was still home, and even though I felt more "me" in Singapore, I hadn't been able to articulate it, nor did I really understand it. After all, England had adopted me as one of its own. As a child, I even had dreams of representing England at rugby and aspired more to be like Rob Andrew rather than Rory Underwood, the latter being of mixed Malaysian-English heritage.

That 2014 trip to Singapore had rekindled something in me. More than a love or respect for the country, I felt a connection. It was like a homing beacon had been turned on and, even though I was away and enjoying life in the UK, it was pulsing in the background of my heart, slowly getting stronger and brighter as the months and years went by. Our "once in a lifetime" trip to Singapore became annual, returning in 2015 with our new-born daughter, Aspen, and again in 2016. With each trip, we got to know different areas and aspects of Singapore; each time, we became more familiar with the country and culture; each time it felt more like home to all of us. Finally in 2018, I applied for a job at an international school and successfully gained the post. For me, it felt like a ticket home; for Millie it was the realisation of a four-year dream, and so when it all fell through in the summer, we were devastated. Both Millie and I had handed in our notices at our places of work and both employers had already found our replacements, and so we were left jobless and homeless.

Hope came in the form of a job back in my childhood county of Surrey, south of London, and just two weeks later our little family of four moved house. The three-and-a-half hour journey was filled with mixed emotions of sadness and anticipation for the future. Surrey treated us well and I had the chance to reconnect with some friends with whom I grew up. A year went by without us considering a move to Singapore as we decided that, for our own mental health (and that of our children), we needed to feel settled, at least for a little while, but the homing beacon continued to shine brighter than ever. We decided to renew the hunt for jobs but few opportunities came up. One of the few available jobs even felt like the one, and I can still feel the pain and disappointment of narrowly missing out. I was at work when I found out. An emotional person, I did well to hold it together for the rest of the day and all the way home. I arrived home while Millie was out at a park with the kids and went to the kitchen to make myself a coffee. She had left me a handwritten note on a square of lined paper next to the coffee machine, which read:

"Please don't feel bad about the job, love. The dream will happen and when it does, it will be amazing. I love you. x"

The floodgates opened. I cried an uncontrollable cry. You know, the sort of ugly cry you smother in a pillow so you don't catch an unfortunate glimpse of yourself in the mirror. I was lucky that no one was home and that we lived in the countryside. The note lived on the fridge until the day we finally moved to Singapore.

* * *

We were at church when the job offer finally came. Millie and I were the kids' pastors of our local church, a big church, with around 200 kids every Sunday. We met at the civic centre, a venue with an auditorium that sat 1000 people and it regularly hosted concerts, plays and talks. I was in the middle of looking after a group of 65 seven-to-eleven year olds when an email vibrated my phone in my pocket. "Please may we have a Skype call in 15 minutes? I can't really make any other time today." Fifteen minutes?! That was exactly when all the parents came to collect the children, the busiest part of a Sunday! I was so grateful that we had a fantastic team of capable volunteers, which meant I could take the call. I was in a hoodie and a baseball cap—not really the attire for a final interview, but I had only been given 15 minutes notice, right? I swapped jumpers with Millie and even though hers was a little small, it wouldn't be obvious on a video call. I took my hat off and tried to give my hair a bit of volume and then went outside.

I sat on a bench in the street and waited for the call. My face was cold: it was January 2020, but the low winter sun warmed the black jumper on my chest. I remember it as if it happened just this morning. The man on the other end of the call was an American and he was friendly and kind. His offer of the job came with other reassurances, like my children's education and health insurance, and the way he spoke made me trust he was telling the truth—and he was. While I still needed to await finalisation of a contract, I knew that whatever was laid out in it was our ticket to Singapore. I was going home after 33 years of being away. I walked back into the civic centre with a huge smile on my face, excitement and adrenaline threatening to burst out of my body. Millie was in charge of ensuring the children were checked out and returned to their parents safely and the queue of parents had already filled the bright, sunlit foyer. I stood close to her and quietly said in her ear, "It's time to pack your bag." She turned to look me in the eye, hers lighting up and growing wide. I smiled. We knew we couldn't speak about it at that moment and I needed to sit down and process what had just happened.

The venue had a spacious and comfortable Green Room for its performers and our church used it as a team lounge. Valuing its large volunteer body, the church provided coffee and snacks there for those who were giving their time over the course of the Sunday. I went in and sat down. Before I had a moment to start thinking about anything the Pastor, Rich Louis, walked in. Rich and I go way back. In fact, our connection stretches further back than our own lives as our grandfathers were friends in Singapore in the 1950s. His dad is a Singaporean who grew up with my parents—our parents are still good friends and have holidayed together recently. "How are you doing, mate?" Rich asked. We rarely had the chance to catch up on a Sunday, but this opportunity came at the perfect time. I relayed my news to him and he was so happy for us. He had known that it was in our hearts to move to Singapore and he not only understood, but he fully supported us. It felt good to tell a friend straight away.

* * *

February passed with increasingly concerning news of the COVID-19 global pandemic. The news channels in the UK showed footage of the army on the streets in Bergamo, Italy, and parades of coffins being brought out as a result of the devastating impact of the virus. The reporters interviewed a local nurse who sobbed as she explained that they were caring for, treating and burying their own colleagues and friends. Tears rolled down my face as I watched in disbelief and my concerns grew as the virus reached the UK. I have a reputation for being easily moved to tears—something I have learned to embrace and value—a strength in empathy, rather than a weakness of emotion. In March, schools closed, forcing teaching to move online, along with church services, live entertainment and friendships. We were so fortunate that Millie was only scheduled to go into work once every two or three weeks, with her role as a teaching assistant being largely redundant because of online learning. It meant that while I was teaching from our little office upstairs in our home, she was downstairs, helping our children with their learning. Like so many other parents at the time, Millie quickly got into a routine of feeding, educating and playing with our kids—all this, while also selling up furniture and other "stuff" that we were not going to need in Singapore. We were happy to start our new home as a blank canvas.

Working from home for me meant that lunchtimes were free from school duties and I loved being able to eat with my kids, or to take them for a woodland walk near our home. Milo and Aspen love climbing trees and playing in the woods. I really love spending time with my family. It seems obvious to say, but I am lucky that while some spend time with their kids to parent them, I really gain so much from them spending time with me. During the lockdown, we found a rhythm and we appreciated our time together.

The UK government limited its people to leaving home only to buy essentials, or to exercise just once a day. Before those regulations were in place, I would only exercise twice or maybe three times a week, but this small allowance made us realise the freedom we had beforehand and we took advantage of our quota. Daily exercise became mandatory in our household. When I started my daily runs, it was amazing—the community seemed to rally together, smiling and giving a nod or a friendly "good afternoon!" as I ran past others using up their exercise quota, either on a walk or a run. But as the days passed and the death toll rose, so did the toll on people's mood and ultimately, their mental health. Less people went out of their homes, and fewer of them were smiling. In times like this, it is easy to feel a little helpless, perhaps hopeless, but for some reason I always feel like I can—and must—do something. My sentiments are expressed far more articulately than I could ever pen them in this inspiring quote of Edward Everett Hale:

"I am only one, but still I am one. I cannot do everything, but still I can do something. And because I cannot do everything, I will not refuse to do the something that I can do."

My "something" was to go running around our village three or four times a week dressed as a giant banana (it's amazing what you have in the cupboards when you are a kids' pastor!) in order to put a smile on people's faces during this challenging time. Anonymity is a strange thing. The first time I ran out of my home I felt like a complete lunatic, embarrassed, even though no one knew it was me. The uncontrollable smile on my face was more out of embarrassment than anything else, but as villagers began to smile back, wave and even laugh out loud, the purpose behind my silly fruit costume-wearing runs would come into sharp focus and so I continued to do it for 25 runs, running a total of over 150km. Anonymity made it easy to keep doing it, and it also meant I could pass the costume on to another anonymous runner to continue the craze. During this time I remained aware of the impact of COVID-19 across the globe, particularly in Singapore, but while the situation was largely under control, I was ignorant of the negative impact it was having on the world of international schools.

It was a Wednesday morning and I woke up with an email in my inbox from the school in Singapore, asking for a Skype call just two hours later. I looked at my schedule for the day and it was clear. The wording of the email was professional—it didn't hint at anything either positive or negative, but I had a horrible feeling in my gut that I tried to suppress as I told Millie I had a call with Singapore. The kids were in the garden at the time of the call. I shut the door to our little office and sat down to log on. There were four of us on the call: the Superintendent, the Principal, the HR director and me. Due to the global pandemic, more students were having to leave the school and so the school needed to cut staff to match the intake. My job was gone. The others on the call were understanding and I could tell they genuinely felt horrible about having to share this news. I mean, it's not the sort of news anyone wants to share. They thanked me for my grace. I wondered if I should have fought harder, but really, I knew it was non-negotiable.

My mind turned towards how I would tell Millie and the kids. Twice getting the job, twice resigning from a great post, now twice it had fallen through. Were we ever going to make it to Singapore? The advantage of having been through the same thing before was that we knew what to do. We remained calm. Inside, my heart was screaming, outside… well, outside, I didn't know what to feel. I tried hard to think clearly about what to do next. I went online and looked for jobs, both international and local. But this was the peak of COVID-19, it was already late May and I was looking for a job to start August or September. There were three jobs. Thailand, Dubai and the UK. I applied for all of them, closed the laptop and prayed.

As the hours and days went by I would open my laptop and check my emails in case they somehow didn't come through on my phone. I would sit and hit refresh every few minutes on job websites to see if another opportunity in Singapore would appear. Nothing. I became fluent at checking the time in the UK, calculating what time it was in Singapore—knowing that by the time it reached 11am, there was very little hope of anything else coming up that day. It was a Sunday afternoon, 2.52pm—almost 10pm in Singapore—when an email came through. "We'd like to have a video call with you tomorrow morning…" It was the same school that had told me there was no vacancy—could they have made a mistake? Did they have a job for me after all? My thoughts were all over the place, but I needed to remain realistic and calm. I struggled to sleep that night and morning took forever to arrive. In the UK at the start of June, the sun rises early— around 5.30am. A small crack in our bedroom curtains seemed to illuminate the whole room, even though the sun was only just bringing a bit of colour into the early hours and I couldn't get back to sleep. Days of broken sleep had meant I was super tired, but it made no difference. I went downstairs to make a coffee.

From our kitchen window I could see the mist laying upon the meadow behind our house. Everything was still. I stood there, in the kitchen, looking out of the window for a long time. I settled my heart for whatever was to come and prayed. Faith is a funny thing. It kicks into play when there is a metaphorical mountain ahead or if you're in the middle of a storm. It helps to navigate the highs and lows of life and gives one the ability to trust that everything will be better. Some call it a crutch. I guess it is in a way—a crutch gives strength and stability to those who are too weak to go it alone.

Our kids were incredible during the lockdown, but even then they had their moments. That Monday morning was one of those moments and so Millie decided she would take them for their daily exercise just before my video call. The house was silent, yet still I felt the need to close the door. Perhaps I felt like I needed the safety and comfort of a closed door. The call came and they cut right to the chase. They had created a very similar role for me in a different part of the school—an older age group—which was a role I preferred. "Please have a think about this option and let us know within the next 24 hours if it suits you." I didn't need the time. I accepted straight away. Millie, of course, was overjoyed. We had made the decision to refrain from telling the children that things had fallen through, and that we would explain to them what was happening when we knew we had a solid plan. This proved to be the right decision, for as far as they were concerned, nothing had changed—we were still moving to Singapore.

We spent the next four weeks frantically getting ready to move, filling in what felt like endless paperwork with brand

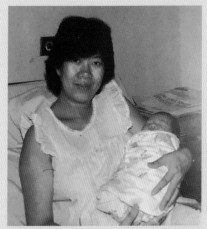

My mother holds me at just a few days old.

My older sister, Charmaine and me at 2 months old.

My old apartment in Ang Mo Kio, I wonder how my parents felt bringing me home that day?

Nine months old in my crib in the Ang Mo Kio apartment.

Even at a young age I seemed to enjoy my food as there are many photos of me in my high chair—usually with an empty plate!

Me at 18 months old with my older sister, Charmaine. We were visiting my Grandma who was working in Australia at the time.

At 12 years old, wearing the David Seaman goalkeepers shirt from Euro '96.

Five years old. My younger sister Amanda is sporting the tie, with Charmaine in the middle and me on the right.

When I was 13 years old, rugby and sport had become my passion.

Millie and me at Rome's Trevi Fountain, whilst on honeymoon in 2011.

Four generations of Tan men, taken in 2014 at my parents' home in Marymount.

The Flower Dome at Gardens by the Bay—our first trip as a little family in 2014, the first time I felt like my homing beacon had been activated.

Dressed as a banana on one of my 25 runs during the COVID lockdown in the UK.

Aspen and I look out of our quarantine window (July 2020), dreaming of what's to come.

Arrival in Singapore and our reunion with my grandparents.

new COVID regulations, selling the last few bits we were not going to take and trying to find time to say goodbye to friends. We were sad knowing we were leaving friends, but despite the difficulties, each goodbye was coated with the joy of our pending move across the globe. The last few days were spent with a wonderful family and good friends, Paul and Ruth. We had only known each other for two years, but we had connected like we had been friends forever, bonding over late night chats and great food. They treated us like VIPs in their home, welcoming my parents and my younger sister and her family for meals in our final few days, and even throwing a birthday celebration for Milo, who enjoyed a ride on the back of Paul's Harley Davidson as a birthday treat. He loved it.

* * *

We flew out on Milo's birthday, 6th July, and he was so excited about being on a plane and having unlimited snacks and screen time to celebrate. Our flight was empty. The continued global rise of COVID-19 cases meant that international travel had been hugely restricted and our plane had just 50 passengers. We wore our face masks throughout the 13 hour flight—a new feeling for us, given that the UK's regulations at the time did not require masks. We arrived at Singapore's Changi Airport and had a brief moment to take in the humid air—the feeling of home—before being whisked away onto a coach that took us to a hotel for our 14-day quarantine. It provided a timely opportunity for us to rest and regroup. It had been a mad four weeks of paperwork, packing, selling and dumping.

Our final days in the UK had been tense, as we still had to await permission to fly from the Singapore Government as a temporary COVID-19 measure to limit the numbers of foreign arrivals. With UK travel restrictions in play, we had limited chances to say goodbye to friends and family at a distance—we didn't get to see so many people we value and this, on one hand, made it easier, but on the other hand, so much harder. Each goodbye was emotionally exhausting and each non-goodbye was also emotionally exhausting. So to be forced into doing nothing for 14 days, meals delivered and nothing but TV and a window view, was perfect. To think of our quarantine as our final hurdle was a little strange, as I have never thought that sitting down and relaxing for two weeks would be a challenge. But as we got closer to the end of the two weeks, the desire to give up our rest and get on with life grew stronger. That final morning we woke and it was a relief to know we had made it. Despite being cooped up in a hotel room for two weeks, we managed to avoid any big arguments—in fact, I think we got away without any little arguments too—just good family bonding time. With two days remaining Millie and I were allowed out—separately—to go and have our COVID tests. I had to wear my mask and the taxi driver who took me to my test centre was advised to wind the windows down to ensure a good circulation of fresh air. He kept apologising, but the fresh, warm tropical air in my lungs was a welcome change to the recycled, air-conditioned version in the hotel.

The taxi driver pulled up to a medical centre and I was greeted by many workers in full protection gear. The yellow plastic outfits, face visors and masks were a little intimidating and brought the harsh reality of a global pandemic uncomfortably into view. The staff were friendly, but clearly kept their distance. There was no waiting or queuing up—I went straight to a boothed area, sat down and was asked a few health questions. I had to explain that I'd suffered a rugby injury a number of years ago that had left me with a titanium plate on my right cheekbone and a wire running through my eye socket and so the nurse testing me was extra cautious when testing my right nostril. The swab was long—I considered for a moment if they were planning on swabbing my brain.

Both Millie and I tested negative and at noon on our fourteenth day, we were free. Walking out of the hotel was an amazing feeling. Freedom. Singapore welcomed us with a sunny day. The warm, humid air filled my lungs. We had made it.

* * *

Five months later and here I was, sitting on a bench in Ang Mo Kio, a resident in my country of birth for the first time in 34 years, taking in the sights, smells, feeling, taste and sounds of the neighbourhood. There was also a deeper sense—of home, belonging and a fulfilment. I have felt fulfilment for many years, through my job, my family and purpose, but this one was different. My father had described this HDB block to me over the phone and amazingly, I saw it within moments of walking out of the MRT station. The bench I sat on provided me with a view of the neighbourhood and the community. I watched street cleaners collect the tiniest bits of litter from the floors, as well as decanting trash from trash cans into a bag. I have since learned that this is to reduce unnecessary plastic wastage. People walked their dogs. Others walked by having been to the market. Buses drove past and every few minutes I could hear a train go by. It was morning time and despite the quieter train at the start of the day, the town was beginning to come alive.

I wasn't sure what to expect. I didn't know what I'd feel. All I knew was that I had a strong sense that Singapore felt more like home to me than the UK and I wanted to understand why. After all, I had only lived in Singapore, in Ang Mo Kio, for less than two years. Did those two years create such a strong impression upon my infant brain that it has stuck with me all these years? What was it that provided such a strong connection? Why did it feel like home? While I didn't feel like I was missing anything, I did feel like there was so much to be discovered. I was visiting the block where I lived as an infant and decided to take the lift to our old apartment. I knew I wouldn't be able to go in—it was someone else's home now, but I wanted to see the front door. I wanted to experience where I had lived and the surrounding environment. Looking at the front door was nice and I stared at it for a few minutes. I tried to imagine my mother and father bringing me home. I remember feeling so out of my depth when we first brought Milo home from the hospital. I felt like we needed to sign something to say we had received him in good order and it was strange walking out of the hospital having not been given an instruction manual, or at least a quick tutorial on how to care for a baby. Along with that feeling, I can clearly remember the pride I had when coming home that day with my son. In fact, I felt the same with Aspen—our second child, but a wholly different sense of pride over my little girl. I could picture my dad holding me while trying to open the gate, and what it must have been like for them coming home with two children. I wondered what memories my parents had behind that door and what milestones I achieved just a few metres away. My first words would have been spoken in there. This is the place where I learned to walk.

At the top of that apartment block was a VIP viewing deck. Queen Elizabeth II had even visited and enjoyed the view in 1989. I thought I would go and see if it was open to the public, or whether it was still very exclusive, so I took the lift up to the top floor. The door to the observation deck no longer had royal appeal. It needed a lick of paint and was padlocked. I gave it a wriggle to see if it was unlocked, or loose. It stood firm. Two of the residents on the floor had their doors open and were talking with each other. It turns out Singapore's Housing Development Board (HDB) who own the apartment blocks were carrying out essential updates to the whole block and so both neighbours decided that it would be an appropriate time to have renovations and were sharing the services of the builders. They were very friendly and asked me if I was OK, if I needed any help with anything? I explained why I was there and that I was hoping to get to the observation deck. To my gratitude and amazement, I was invited into their homes to experience the view "just a few metres below the observation deck". I had a camera with me, and they gave me space and time to film and take some shots. The lady explained what I would have been able to see from my apartment when I was a baby. I tried to imagine myself in my parents arms, looking out over the neighbourhood, the sun rising over the horizon. I was then taken through to the other neighbour's apartment to see the view from there. Looking down from the gentleman's window, I could see the MRT station and a lush green park nestled among the apartment blocks. The apartment was clearly in the middle of renovations, furniture stacked, dust sheets covering the piles of precious belongings. I tried to take everything in, to bank it in my memory, but it was hard to do without seeming nosy. I tried to remember the layout of the home, the tiled floor and the safety bars on the windows, and I tried to imagine "baby me" crawling around on the floor, playing with my older sister.

Not wanting to overstay my welcome, I thanked the neighbours many times and made my way downstairs. Singapore tends to wake up in shifts. At around 7.30am the MRT trains are jam-packed with commuters heading to office jobs and students going to school. Then there is a lull until about 10.30am when local shops start opening. It was about 10.30am when I headed down. I walked further into the HDB area, "bathing" in the environment. Hawker centres, to me, have two smells. One of food and irresistible flavours that will make you hungry regardless of when you last ate. The other smell is a morning smell. It's a mix of coffee and something else. The something else is a combination of produce that has been cleaned out from the day before, the dewy smell of Singapore's morning air and maybe the smell of wiped-down tables. It's hard to describe. But it's familiar and I could smell it as I wandered around the neighbourhood, so I headed towards the hawker centre.

"Good morning, aunty! One kopi and one char siew bao, please!" I said in a slightly raised voice. In Singapore, older generations are referred to as *aunty* or *uncle* as a sign of respect. It also adds to the sense of family and community, I guess. There's a hum of noise—the polyphony of fans, traffic and general ambience of a hawker centre.

"Two dollar!" Came the response and I handed over a $2 note with both hands. This was a new habit—a sign of respect. I took my small brunch and sat down. The hawker centre was quiet. Plastic chairs surrounded round tables and the ceiling fans blew my napkin. I trapped it under my plate. Taste. I had watched, listened, felt and smelt the area around me and now it was time to sit and taste. A sixth sense was rising too. A sense of home. It was strange, I felt completely relaxed in that place. Not just relaxed, but content. Also, might I just add, coffee and a bao for $2. This may seem like a small and insignificant fact—certainly the cost will be no surprise to Singaporeans—but for me, affordable and easily accessible food and drink and a place to sit and enjoy them is one of the things that makes Singapore such a wonderful place to live. It is a feature of Singaporean life that easily facilitates community. It means that an office worker can grab a quiet drink after his or her busy day to switch off before going home to a family. It means that teenagers can sit and chat in a safe environment and it means that pensioners can sit and enjoy a drink and company, too.

It had been six years since that first time I felt like Singapore was home. Six years since that homing beacon had been turned on. That morning I had only spent a couple of hours in Ang Mo Kio, but it had shown me so much about my first home and community. I found out that the welcoming sense of community that I had was valued in this neighbourhood. No one told me—I just felt it: the warmth of the neighbours who invited me into their homes; the way people interacted with each other. It was very clear to me. Even the feelings I had that I couldn't articulate created clarity in my mind and heart. What I experienced in Ang Mo Kio that morning was a microcosm of the wider Singapore, a country with not just shared values, but a country of unity. I was grateful to be back, to be a resident and to be contributing to its society. It had been a good introduction to my new (and old!) home, but I felt aware that there were many layers of my home that I did not know, many layers that I hadn't ever uncovered. I was also aware that while I felt local, I was in fact an immigrant and largely ignorant of everyday life in Singapore, of its culture and its history. What I did know was that I had begun a journey of self-discovery and I was looking forward to exploring the hidden treasures of my heritage and of Singapore's DNA, its values and its personality.

Chapter 2

Pilgrimage

It has been said that to know a country you must walk its streets, meet its people and eat its food. As someone who loves hiking, socialising and eating, perhaps it is no surprise that I love to travel and explore cities, countries and cultures. Over the years I have had the honour of visiting over 20 nations and meeting, experiencing and befriending people from all over the world. I love searching out the local boulangerie in quaint French villages and witnessing the breathtaking coastline of Italy's Amalfi Coast. I will never forget seeing Maasai people going about their daily lives in Tanzania and the warmth and kindness of the Slovakian people. It would be easy to assume, after being born in Singapore (as a Singaporean!) and then returning for holidays maybe 10 or 11 times, that I already know everything about Singapore and its people—but this just isn't the case, and so I began thinking of a way I could explore the country and perhaps quickly gain a knowledge. This is when the idea of a pilgrimage came to mind.

A pilgrimage is a journey that someone takes to a place unknown to them in order to find something new about the land and about themselves, often with a spiritual element, too. There are many famous pilgrimages around the world and I have never been on one. I have visited the Vatican City in Rome, but wasn't there on pilgrimage. We used to live near Walsingham in the east of England—a major pilgrimage destination for Catholics, but we never experienced it on Pilgrim's Day. I would love to visit Israel one day, but that day hasn't yet come. I am drawn to the idea of some other pilgrimages, too: Japan's Kumano Kodo and the 500km St. Paul Trail in Turkey among them.

Singapore isn't really a land well-known for pilgrimages. The only pilgrimage I am aware of in Singapore—and there may be others—is the annual pilgrimage to Kusu Island (Tortoise Island). Perhaps the reason why there aren't any well-known pilgrimages in Singapore is because there aren't really any unknown parts of the country and no hard-to-navigate areas—everywhere is accessible by a train, bus or taxi. To add to that, Singapore is a small country (the 20th smallest in the world) and, to me anyway, a pilgrimage needs to have some distance to it, otherwise it's just a walk in the park. It is, I believe, the inconvenience and challenge that adds to the journey and experience of a pilgrim.

In my attempts to get to know Singapore a little better as a new resident, I joined a few Facebook groups. It was on one of these Facebook groups where I first heard of the Singapore Round Island Route (SRIR): a series of 15 checkpoints around the circumference of the country, spanning 150km. Every few days, photos of people reaching more checkpoints, or completing the SRIR, would come through to my phone. It was inspiring to hear of the experiences of the various hikers (the local cyclists have their own version, which they call the Round

Island Route, or RTI). People of all generations were popping on a pair of trainers and setting out of their homes, discovering areas of their country they had never visited before. This got me excited to explore too, and for some reason I had the idea to try to complete the full Round Island Route in one shot. 150km is much more than I had ever walked or run, but for some reason, I seemed to be able to justify it in my over-confident and naïve mind. It should be OK, right? I didn't think about it for too long before I committed to it.

I wouldn't normally call myself impulsive. I love challenges and I enjoy pushing myself to achieve, particularly with something physical. I love playing sports, both team and individual, and I really enjoy outdoor activities like kayaking, bouldering and hiking. In 2018, I climbed Mount Kilimanjaro, Africa's tallest mountain. The experience was one I will never forget. The varied landscapes of Kilimanjaro were like nothing I had ever seen and the people I met—the climbers on my team and the porters who supported us—were all amazing. I had never felt so physically challenged in my life—a combination of tiredness and altitude sickness, from which I suffered badly. I took in the staggering views and the unfamiliar landscapes, learning from the local porters about the native trees and stories about the mountain.

I asked on the Facebook group if there was anyone who had done the Singapore Round Island Route in one go, so I could ask them for advice on my own attempt. I received many replies, but no one said they had done it, nor did they know anyone who had even attempted it (although I know a few have completed it since). A few sceptics made jokes: "Someone tried it before and his final checkpoint was the Singapore General Hospital!" Unfortunately, I am one of those people for whom being told "it's not possible" makes me want to do something even more. So, ignorantly, I went into this single-stage Round Island Route trek, aiming to complete it in 30 hours.

It was a multi-faceted hike. In the UK, Millie and I would go into the mountains two or three times a year and enjoy the nature, challenge and relative solitude of the British countryside. We had planned on exploring the mountains and countryside of Malaysia, but due to COVID-19 regulations, we were unable to travel and, while Singapore has much to offer in outdoor experiences, Bukit Timah hill doesn't really compare to the Lake District, Snowdonia or the Highlands of the UK, let alone Mount Kilimanjaro or other larger mountain ranges of the world. Part of the motivation behind the hike was a chance for me to get away. Not so much into nature, but to experience a bit of solitude. As well as really enjoying socialising, I find that some time alone often helps me to reset—to clear my head, organise my thoughts and to refresh. I had planned on doing it a few days before Christmas 2020 and we had been going solidly since July without a chance for me to process the move, my new job, or living in a new country. I also wanted to bring a bit of awareness to a fantastic charity, the YWCA, who, through the efforts of willing and dedicated volunteers, provide up to 500 meals a day to people in need. So I used the platform of this hike to share their wonderful work and to encourage people to donate to their cause. The final aspect of the hike, for me, was pilgrimage: a chance to learn something new about my country and myself.

I spent time over the course of about 10 days planning my route and laid it all in a spreadsheet. I really like spreadsheets. By the time I proposed to Millie, I had put together a spreadsheet of all the features she had described that she wanted to include on her wedding day. I had collated telephone numbers, websites and quotes. When she said "yes" to my one-knee-in-the mud, cold, January afternoon proposal, I was able to present her with this document. Our wedding was pretty much planned with no issues within two weeks!

The hiking spreadsheet included checkpoints—official and unofficial—which would serve as landmarks. I had calculated how long it should take from each checkpoint and what time I would reach certain places. I had listed all of my kit, highlighted where I would stop for food and where I would fill up water and I had planned what time I would be walking certain stretches in case friends were keen to join me. I would start at Palawan Beach on Sentosa, cross the footbridge boardwalk onto the main island and walk clockwise around it, completing the hike at the top of Mount Faber, which, despite its name, is only 106 metres high. By this stage, our YouTube channel, WONDERLUST, had begun to gain some popularity and so we decided that I would film this journey for an episode.

I sat on my bed and laid out all my gear. This had become a ritual before expeditions and hikes. It is a good way for me to look at everything that is going into my bag and to check that I have everything I need. I also use the opportunity to picture the scenarios in which I will need certain things and to mentally prepare for the journey. This pack list was slightly different to previous ones. I had to bring a lot more food than before. While I knew there were hawker centres and food courts, I didn't want to spend time queuing for meals, and much of the route didn't pass food stops, or was during the night. So I had to pack some food. I used fajita wraps filled with ham and cheese, tightly wrapped in tin foil. There was no sleeping bag or ground mat, as I wasn't planning on sleeping, and these were replaced by two cameras and a drone. The thought of red-raw blisters was not one that filled me with joy and so I also packed a spare set of trainers in case of a heavy downpour. Knowing too well Singapore's heat, I loaded in a three-litre bladder of water, a bottled isotonic drink and some salts, to replace what I'd likely loose in sweat. I packed everything into my bag and felt ready.

I felt optimistic about my pilgrimage and its challenge as I strapped my bag onto my back. I love putting on a backpack. It is a familiar and happy feeling that usually precedes an adventure. The backpack I chose for this trip was my favourite one and it was adorned with patches from various mountain trips. It felt heavy with five litres of fluids as well as my food for the journey and the camera gear, but I felt strong and was certain that once I started on my trek, the adrenaline would kick in and I wouldn't even feel the weight. We took the train to Singapore's Harbourfront, where we crossed over to Sentosa Island by monorail. Sentosa is a small island—just 5km wide—and is set up as a giant holiday resort. When I was a kid, I heard one of my uncles say that Sentosa stands for "So Expensive—Nothing To See Also". That may have been the case back then, but nowadays it is filled with hotels and attractions, and a cross-island cable car has recently been installed to complement the monorail we took that day. There was a bit of a walk from the monorail station to the starting point on Palawan Beach and I felt I should have added these kilometres to my complete target of 153.6km.

Somehow Singapore's main newspaper, *The Straits Times*, had gotten word about my hike and they sent along a photographer to mark the start of the journey. I had invited my friend, Eric, who happens to be an award-winning film producer, to come along and take some drone shots of Palawan Beach. He had generously taken time out of his busy schedule to come down. I passed him the drone when the staff at the beach stopped us. "You are not allowed to fly drones here", said the beach entry official.

"I checked the regulations and it says that Palawan Beach is a free-to-fly zone", I remarked, confidently, having checked all of the rules and regulations online. The beach entry official looked at his colleagues, who also seemed unsure.

"I think you must have special permission as Sentosa is classified as private property—we cannot allow you to fly your drone here."

I was frustrated, at the *I think*—nothing definite—but decided to play it cool, apologising to Eric, who had made such an effort to help. *The Straits Times* photographer complained about the inconsistencies of the rules as he had been on the same beach using a drone a few weeks earlier, but neither he, nor Eric, were surprised.

"In Singapore it is always a 'no' unless the highest authority says 'yes'," said the heavy-set photographer.

"It's OK, I don't mind too much," I replied. Despite his kindness, the photographer was the most bothered by the ruling as we walked across the warm, white sand to the starting point. It was a very sunny day and it was hard to keep my eyes open without squinting due to the sunshine. He had me pose on the beach in the sunshine and then on some rocks in the shade before wishing me luck and heading on his way.

4.44pm. I watched the second hand edge towards the 12. And I was off. The pilgrimage had begun. Immediately, I began to feel sand enter my shoe and I could hear the advice of many mountaineers telling me to take my shoes off and tap out the sand before continuing any further, but I felt that stopping 40 metres into the journey, while Millie and Eric were filming, wasn't very professional. I think I also felt the pressure of Eric's accolades, so I decided I would wait until I had passed everyone and was on my own before dealing with the sand. Fortunately the decision was not detrimental to my walk.

The boardwalk that bridges Sentosa to Singapore's main island was much shorter than I remember. The last time we walked on it, we saw a big ray of some sort jump out of the water and splash down. I kept a weather eye on the water, hoping to catch a glimpse of something, but I was less fortunate this time. My colleague and friend, Ben, met me on the other side of the boardwalk. Ben set off at a solid pace and I had to ask him to slow down a little. I had told a few colleagues that I was going to attempt this hike around Singapore and asked if any of them would be keen to join me for a section of the route. Quite casually, Ben said "I'd be keen to join you for the whole thing!"

I was a little surprised, but he looked fit and was Canadian. The Canadian element, to me, counted for a lot. I have only met a few Canadians in my time, but they all seemed to have a comfort in the outdoors and a penchant for more extreme hikes and expeditions, and so I was excited to have Ben join me on the journey.

We headed west, aiming for the Henderson Waves bridge. I had never been there before, although I had seen pictures. As we approached, I was taken aback by how high the bridge was off the ground—and it seemed to get taller the closer we got—something I like to call the Eiffel Tower syndrome. In Paris, you can see the Eiffel Tower at many different points. It seems tiny from a distance, like the Eiffel Tower keyrings you can buy, but as you get closer, it gets bigger and bigger. Eventually, you think you have seen the magnitude of it but even in the last 200 metres, it seems to grow even more. The Henderson Waves bridge was just like that.

We walked up the stairs from ground level to get to the start of the bridge. The opening of the bridge was quite unassuming, it didn't feel like we were up so high, or that there would be a large drop appearing any time soon. I imagined how it would have looked before the modernisation of Singapore. Rainforest canopy overhead, crowding the light away from ground level, thick vegetation limiting your vision moving forward. The drop where the bridge juts out of the hill would have been easy to miss and I wonder how many people had slipped and fallen. It was quite an experience to walk out onto that bridge. I have been on higher bridges in equally, and arguably, much more beautiful places before. Most notably, the Millau Viaduct, in the South of France, which stands a staggering 270 metres above the ground below and offers quite a stunning view of the valley below. We drove over it in 2017 on our way to our holiday destination in a village called Vinassan not far from Narbonne and Perpignan. We were running about 30 minutes behind schedule which, when your aim is to arrive in time for a late breakfast having driven through the night, puts pressure on the driver of a car full of hungry passengers. Still, we had to stop on the tallest bridge in the world and experience the light, wispy clouds, resting upon the surrounding landscape. Although much smaller, the Henderson Waves held its own majesty. We paused to take in the view, and could see Sentosa in the distance. The "waves" of the bridge mimic the Southern Ridges, a 10km stretch of low hills in which the award-winning bridge stands. Its smooth wooden curves create a sense of it growing and twisting out of the rainforests and I enjoyed the walk across.

Our first target checkpoint was to reach the West Coast Park at around sunset to meet Millie and the kids. Ben didn't pack food to eat along the way and so we were going to stop at the McDonalds for him to grab some dinner. There I was having carefully calculated my calories and then there was Ben, casually re-fuelling on a burger and fries. The task ahead seemed much lighter to Ben, and I was concerned that I was going to slow him down and disappoint. We entered West Coast Park as dusk settled and it felt good to be running close to the planned schedule. I could hear the sound of a pressure washer. In the UK, when we wanted to get our car cleaned, we would take it to a run-down looking garage behind a pub in our village and leave our car and its keys with the team of four or five Eastern Europeans to clean our car. As I would walk away towards a cafe to have a coffee while I waited, I could always hear the sound of the dirt on my car being aggressively attacked by a jet spray. I could hear that same sound in the park, but it wasn't coming from a car wash—no! It was coming from a vending-machine car-wash hybrid, designed for cleaning dogs! And there was a queue! People were lining up after dark to clean their dogs! I suppose there isn't a lot of space in Singapore's apartments to be able to bathe one's dog and so it makes complete sense, but I had never experienced one before and so it provided some novelty.

We met Millie and the kids, who were playing in a fairly expansive playground, which had well-maintained apparatus that grew out of gigantic sand pits and was filled with kids of all ages laughing and having fun. It was 8pm and in the UK, kids would be getting ready for bed and the slightly threatening characters of the night would be coming out—not in every park, but in the evenings, playgrounds don't have the safe and fun atmosphere they do in the daytime. Come to think of it, I don't know whether many play parks in the UK are lit well enough to accommodate night-time play. A large number of playgrounds in Singapore were commissioned in the 1970s to intentionally create a space for community to be built between the varying races and cultures that call Singapore home. Now, half a century later, I can see that this was a successful move. Families were enjoying their time outside and in stark contrast to Singapore's MRTs, there were no phones in hands and no screen-illuminated faces. There was a beautiful sense of community around us. Chinese, Indians, Malays—I even heard French being spoken as some Caucasian kids ran past. Our own mixed-heritage kids were playing amongst the skin kaleidoscope and their different hues were not out of place—it just added to the colour and the beauty. I loved the blend and wondered whether kids see skin colour or whether they see people. The kids were having so much fun playing that when it was time for Ben and me to continue on our way, there was only a brief goodbye.

In England, my parents live in a converted old barn in the middle of nowhere. The nearest town is 6 miles (9.6km) away and there are no streetlights. During winter, the sun sets at around 4pm and the darkness settles in until about 8am the next day. Stars glow on the velvet black skies, and if you wait out in the dark for a good 20 minutes, your eyes adapt to the darkness and billions of shining specks seem to take off their invisibility cloaks as they appear above. The Singapore night-time has a different hue. It is a glow of whites and yellows, a reflection from the tarmacked roads of the street lights that illuminate the way for the many people who are still awake and active after the sun sets. Stars aren't really visible. Instead, the lights of the night sky are from the windows of high-rise apartment blocks and the skyscrapers in the city's Central Business District. We were heading to the west—an area of Singapore I had not experienced before, with the exception of Jurong Bird Park. Our next target landmark was a lighthouse, the Johor Lighthouse, at the far western point of Singapore. Ben had read in an article that being at the lighthouse felt more like you were in Australia and he was keen to experience it—especially having been stuck in Singapore due to COVID-19 travel restrictions.

We walked through the Pioneer and Tuas areas. My mother used to visit the *kampong* (traditional village) in Tuas, which, at the time, was a fishing village, for her holidays when she was a child. She says she must have had a family friend there, although she can't remember who. The Tuas I experienced that night was a far cry from that of my mother—the *kampong* which would have been made up of corrugated tin-roofed houses raised on stilts, to manage the flooding it used to experience. Instead, it was industrial. Factories, warehouses and industrial workshops lined the streets. Many of these were closed for the day, but a good number were still open and operating into the night, filling the air with a whirring sound of productivity. While life continued in the buildings, the streets became temporary work stations for road workers, setting up floodlights and marking out sections with traffic cones. It was clear that Singapore encouraged night-time road work, allowing the daytime shift to be able to work uninterrupted by traffic hold-ups and diversions. We walked past loud machinery and we were halted by traffic officers, who seemed not to be surprised at two chaps hiking through at that time. I was surprised at the size of the MRT stations, which seemed a colossal height, especially as the vast majority of Singapore's MRT is underground.

Quiet roads continued to be accompanied by lit buildings. It is amazing how clever lighting can mask and highlight all the right parts, making a simple car park look like something from the future. Unfortunately, the lighting was unable to mask some pungent smells that engulfed our faces through the Pioneer area. Being a small nation surrounded by the sea, Singapore does not have many sources of clean, drinkable water, and so currently around 40 per cent of its water is imported through a huge, 1km-long pipeline from Malaysia. This percentage has dropped over the years as Singapore has managed to find new ways of creating clean water, and the country seeks to become completely self-sufficient by 2061, when its 100-year water supply agreement with Malaysia ends. It aims to achieve this by using techniques such as water desalination, improved local supply from its reservoirs and through water reclamation. Water reclamation is a phenomenal method of recycling water. If you're thinking, "eew, that sounds like drinking your pee!", you're absolutely correct. Singapore has found a way to clean every molecule of water and bottle it to make it even cleaner than the water you buy from the shops. The smell that engulfed our senses was the smell of recycled water… just before the purification and recycling bit. What made it worse was that across the road was the oil refinery, which also smelt fairly unrefined!

We consulted our maps as we approached the Johor Straits lighthouse, or the Raffles Marina lighthouse as it is also called. Singapore has five lighthouses that are operated by the government, one famously on the top of an apartment block in Bedok, but the Raffles Marina lighthouse is a privately-owned and -operated lighthouse. We were looking for our taste of Down Under and to experience a hidden gem of Singapore. Ben had lived in Singapore for over a decade and had never visited. The entrance to the Raffles Marina Club, which serves as the gatekeeper to the lighthouse, was closed. It must have been around 11.40pm and the gates were shut and locked by the guards of the exclusive hotel and yacht club at about 10pm. Gutted. In the weeks following this mammoth hike, Millie, the kids and I returned to the Raffles Marina Club to experience the lighthouse and we enjoyed what felt like a very European afternoon, eating fresh (and beautifully cooked) seafood pasta with a view over the stunning multi-million dollar yachts with the lighthouse in the distance. But that night, we were too late— we had missed our chance to see the lighthouse. It was crippling. We had been anticipating the reward of seeing the lighthouse and having a bite to eat while enjoying the view and atmosphere, but instead, we sat in a bus shelter next to an empty road, with the view of MRT trains pulling into the depot at the end of their late-night shift. It magnified the aches and fatigue we were beginning to feel in our feet and legs.

To continue on our journey we had to backtrack through Tuas and we found ourselves winding through parts of the industrial estate to keep the route fresh. Even cutting through back alleys, it felt safe and non-threatening. The noise of factories and construction disappeared, and while the constant hum of traffic remained in the background, there was a peace to the night-time. Fatigue was beginning to settle in and my mind sought a place of focus. I'm not sure when I first entered this mental state, but it's a state I enter when I am feeling physical challenges, usually on hikes or mountain climbs. I remember using it in rugby training when I was younger, getting into a zone of focus when my body is being put through its paces. The last time I dropped into that mindset was a few months earlier on Ben Nevis—the UK's highest mountain. I had brought a friend of mine along for his first experience of the intense contours of the Scottish Highlands. He was fit—a runner—and was storming ahead. Soon after crossing a fast-moving mountain river, we found ourselves on a grassy incline with me 20 metres behind my friend and needing to find that zone to keep pushing on. It is hard to describe when and why I use that mindset—it's not my final bout of energy, it's just a focused zone to push through a physical challenge.

I was in this zone on a long, straight stretch of road when I realised Ben was falling behind. I paused at a bus shelter for him to catch up. "I don't think I'm going to make it," Ben said. He looked tired. His knees and hip were beginning to give him levels of discomfort and we agreed it was safest for him not to continue. It is strange how my initial desire for a chance of solitude was replaced by my enjoyment of good company. I was gutted to be saying goodbye, but I knew it was best for him. Pushing oneself to definite injury is never wise. We walked a little further to a part of the street recognised by Ben's taxi app and we parted ways.

It wasn't long before my Apple Watch started tapping my wrist and I answered to hear a slightly panicked Ben, asking if I was OK. Curious at his startled tones I responded, "I'm fine. Are you OK? What's up?"

"I just saw a pack of wild dogs running in your direction and I wanted to check you were alright," he said, a little concerned.

"I'm alright—I haven't seen any dogs this way. They must have gone in a different direction." I *was* alright—until his call. All of a sudden, I felt on edge, looking around as if I was about to be chased down by a pack of wolves... I really wasn't, and the dogs didn't make an appearance. Stray and wild dogs are not uncommon in Singapore, although the number of them is decreasing due to management systems put in place by the government. I managed to compose myself and within a few minutes I was back on track—momentum and mind.

In the solitude of the night my mind turned towards my wife. Whilst on our honeymoon in Rome, the Italian city of love, I had a sudden realisation that wherever I go, whatever I do, for the rest of my life, Millie would be right there. This may seem obvious to some, probably most, but for someone who loves his own space and had been living on his own for a few years, this was a significant revelation. I can, hand on heart, honestly say that in our 10 years of marriage I have never had the feeling that I wished she wasn't nearby. On the contrary, when I have been away on trips or expeditions, I have missed her very quickly. I missed her that night. She is my greatest supporter, my biggest champion and her smile gives me increased determination and energy. Life is always better with her in it.

The solitude and stillness of the night allowed me to consider the purpose of this pilgrimage. Why do I feel like a Singaporean? Why do I feel like Singapore is home? It would be easy to settle on the fact that I was born in Singapore and learned a Singaporean culture in our family home when I grew up, but for me, it isn't quite as simple as that. Neither of my two sisters feel that Singapore is home. My older sister talks about being in Singapore feeling a bit like going back to your parents' house—it's comfortable, it has an emotional draw, but you know that home is somewhere else. My younger sister lived in Singapore as an adult—her daughter was born in Singapore, but she really didn't have the best time and couldn't wait to move back home to the UK. Each of us, despite growing up in the same household, have very different ideas of where we belong. The understanding of "Third Culture Kids", a term coined by David C. Pollock and Ruth E. Van Reken in their book of that title, is one that helps to explain how my siblings and I can have such differing feelings and ideas of belonging. Ancient Greek philosopher Aristotle said, "Knowing yourself is the beginning of all wisdom." Knowing *how* my sisters and I have such differing feelings about Singapore is just part of understanding myself—I wanted to know the *what* and the *why* behind the *who*. Some of the ideas of belonging are a struggle at times for me, as the only boy (and the only one born in Singapore!), especially because I have not performed National Service.

My feet pounded the ground as I continued, the roads quiet. I passed the Jurong Army Camp, where many fresh 18-year-old Singaporean men would go for their National Service (NS). I love hearing all the army stories of different people of different generations. When I was a kid, my father would talk about his NS experiences: training in the pitch-black jungle, of brutal physical punishment and of great camaraderie. One time, an orange peel was left on the floor in his barracks and because no one owned up to being responsible, the whole platoon had to go for a long run while all holding a part of the one orange peel. It is an experience I have not had and, with it being a mandatory service for all Singaporean men, it is one factor that will probably forever have me questioning my authenticity as a Singaporean.

Despite this, I like to think that there is a lot I can do in service to Singapore—I like to think that our family's YouTube channel, WONDERLUST, is a service to the nation (more on that later); and perhaps in a way, this book serves the nation too, but it really doesn't compare to the two-year sacrifice that Singapore's young men make. Sometimes people ask me if I would do NS if given the chance. Yes. Well, kind of. Having *not* served NS is not something I would necessarily change—in terms of my past and my journey. All of my life's twists and turns, direction and mis-direction, have led me to this point where I am today, and I love my life. The hypothetical is an easy one to answer—and the answer would be yes. Heart-wise, I think it is clear from this book and my thoughts of home, that I would, in a heartbeat, pack my things and shave my head ready to serve. But at 37, I am too old and I am an immigrant—immigrants, understandably, would not have a place in a national army of any sort. It isn't a viable option. So I will continue to serve the nation in other ways.

Some friends had planned on meeting me at the Lighthouse and hike with me for a few hours, but they had pulled out at the last minute, having misunderstood which day I would be there. One of these three friends was very dubious of spending the night-time walking through the Lim Chu Kang Road area as it is lined with cemeteries and he was concerned we may be visited by ghosts. In the UK, hardly anyone would be given the heebie-jeebies about this, but in Singapore there is a greater awareness of the spiritual. During the Hungry Ghost Festival in August, metal incinerators appear on the sidewalks for people to burn paper offerings to their ancestors.

Having never been along Lim Chu Kang Road, I was slightly apprehensive about walking through what I expected to be sketchy, unlit country roads between graveyards. We used to live in the deep countryside in the eastern county of Norfolk in the UK, where the roads were not lit and neighbours were few and far between. I once went out for a run at night-time, and came across some very strange and incredibly close sounds from inside the hedges and trees. I don't think I've ever run 5km as quickly as I did that night. To my surprise, Lim Chu Kang Road was a wide, dead straight, well-lit road. It is so wide, long and straight that it doubles up as an air force runway. It takes less than 48 hours for a team of skilled soldiers to take down the street lights, bus shelters and road signs, and for them to erect safety apparatus and to clear the road of debris so that Singapore's F-15 fighters could take off from and land safely on the road. Walking the Lim Chu Kang Road was peaceful at night-time. There was no one else around. Occasionally a motorcyclist would whizz by, taking advantage of the long stretch of uninterrupted road. My legs were tired and the bus shelters provided a seat for me to sit and have a rest. I could feel blisters on the soles of my feet and I considered popping them to allow my feet to feel a little more comfortable. I left them alone.

The north of Lim Chu Kang Road narrowed into a few smaller roads, with less light. Cars and the odd bus had started to pass— it was perhaps 4.30 or 5am, and so Singapore was starting to wake. As I walked, my feet began to feel numb and the back of my legs were in pain. I looked at the ground and continued to walk, focusing on every step. Out of the corner of my eye, in a badly lit layby, I caught sight of four or five wild dogs. One of them looked like a German Shepherd—all of them looked big. I tried not to notice how hungry they looked as I walked a little quicker. What would happen should I come under attack? My mind flew through so many options—normally my physical strength would give me enough confidence to be able to deal with this situation, but I was exhausted. I felt like the weak buffalo at the back of the herd as a pride of lions were about to attack. Fortunately, I did not need to use my pre-planned self-defence techniques that night and the dogs left me alone. It's a good thing, too, as I don't know how effective poking them in the eyes would have been! I was tired and mentally drained, but the hope of seeing a beautiful sunrise in the northwest of Singapore kept me going. I had heard that sunrises were particularly beautiful at the Kranji Reservoir Park and I was determined to get there. I picked up the pace, lengthening my stride, stretching my muscles as I walked.

Just before I got to Kranji Reservoir Park, I passed Sungei Buloh Wetlands Reserve. It was low light—the sun hadn't broken the horizon yet, but the darkness of night was beginning to fade. The gates to the wetlands reserve were locked. I recalled my relief as my original Google-charted route had required me to navigate through the reserve. I was dubious about hiking through at low-light, as behind those gates was a wild rainforest reserve full of snakes and crocs. I had last been there at the end of 2018, where we came face to face with a king cobra that was casually crossing a footpath. I continued along the road—traffic had begun to pick up a little and teams of cyclists in matching lycra outfits rode past, enjoying the quieter and cooler mornings. My numb feet began to increase their pace as I saw what I thought was the water of the Kranji Reservoir. It wasn't yet sunrise—but it was very close. I skipped across the road, between traffic, into a car park. I had made it. My foot suddenly squelched into a boggy patch of grass. Stepping out of it only made my other foot wet and I realised that the grass in front of me was not going to provide a viable route to the water's edge. I walked round and leant against the metal railing, gazing out across the water. It was a still morning, the water looked like mirror glass, reflecting the bluey purple sky and the silhouettes of the trees around. The horizon turned a golden orange as the morning sun burst through.

I dawdled in a tired haze, taking in the beautiful view while continuing on my journey. I walked along the bridge that separates Kranji Reservoir from the Johor Straits. Fishermen sat there, watching their lines. I couldn't tell whether they looked tired from an early start, or whether they had been there through the night. In the distance I could see Malaysia, a country with which Singapore has a shared history and a country with which I, too, have a closely linked history—my paternal grandpa being born and raised in Malaysia. I sat down, legs throbbing, and the sun began to bring in the energy and activity of a Sunday morning.

I started again, aiming for the Woodlands jetty. I was meeting some friends there and I thought that if I could just make it there, one of them could carry my bag, allowing me to feel a bit lighter. But my legs and feet were hurting. I was limping. In a desperate and tired attempt to burst a blister, I stamped my right foot on the ground, thinking the force would cause a burst, like a balloon. Instead, the skin separated further, increasing the surface area of my blister and causing more pain. I began to realise my ignorance in thinking I could complete 153.6km with very little training or conditioning. I began calculating how long it would take at my reduced pace, and realised that the pace I was going would add a further 24 hours—another night of no sleep. I then started trying to figure out if I had the mental capacity to push through the pain and pick up my speed. I tried it. Nope. My hamstrings felt too tight, like they would snap if I pushed them too hard. I stopped at another bus stop and pulled out my phone. W-O-O-D-L-A-N-D-S... I began typing my next destination into Google maps to see which bus would take me there and as I did, I felt a wave of relief come over me. I needed a break, my legs weren't working and my feet were numb. Just three stops. I toyed with the idea of pushing through and as I finally made the decision to walk the last three stops, the bus showed up and I got on it.

I approached the Woodlands Jetty on a bus. During the ride, I had managed to convince myself that with the help of my friend, Gyuri, carrying my bag, I would be able to make it another 10km to the next checkpoint at Sembawang Hot Spring Park. Singapore has two natural springs: the other one is on Pulau Tekong, a restricted area, only accessible to authorised army personnel. The spring at Sembawang has recently been upgraded from a collection of untidy pipes and taps to a pool with a foot-bathing area and more organised means of accessing fresh spring water. Singapore's obsession with food extends to natural hot springs, and the smell of egg is not from sulphur, but from boiled eggs. Locals bring metal jugs and plastic containers with eggs in them and leave them under the running spring water for a perfectly cooked soft-boiled egg. I had carried in my bag a portable pocket-sized coffee machine, perfect for a cup of espresso with hot spring water, and I was keen to use it for my morning cuppa. That pocket coffee press has been with me on many an expedition, and I particularly love seeing other summiteers catch a whiff of fresh espresso on the top of a mountain. The bus stopped and left me with a 100-metre walk to the jetty, where I was going to meet Gyuri and another colleague, Natasha. Each step was a painful uncomfortable effort. The hopes of getting to Sembawang dwindled as I saw the shock on the faces of my friends. I looked tired and was hobbling.

I stopped and rested for a while. I took off my shoes and patched up my blisters, changing my socks and shoes. I swapped my sweat-dripped t-shirt for a clean one and my body felt fresh. I managed to muster enough energy to get to the car park, where Gyuri and Natasha sent me off home in a taxi. My hike was over and I had managed 74km—less than half of what I had set out to do. I got home, hugged my family and fell asleep for seven hours.

* * *

It took me about two days before I could walk without a hobble or a limp. We were into the monsoon season and so indoor activities were in order—all I could do was walk slowly around a mall and eat some food. I understand that is what a lot of

Singaporeans do at weekends to avoid the heat of the tropical sun, but I was keen to get out and about. The thought of not completing my journey was disappointing and I struggled to shake the feeling of failure and dissatisfaction. I finally decided that I would go to my planned final destination, Mount Faber, to collect my thoughts about my pilgrimage.

I took the cable car up to Mount Faber from Harbourfront Tower 2. COVID regulations meant that I had a cable car to myself, so I took advantage of being on my own and relaxed while taking in the view. On the top of Mount Faber, along with a shop and restaurant, is a bell that used to belong to a Polish ship. It is said that when newlyweds ring the bell together they are guaranteed a lifetime of happiness. There is also a stretch of iron railing that has become the home to an ever-increasing number of little bells. In a similar style to the love locks that were once fastened to le Pont des Arts in Paris, each bell has a wish written on it and it is left on the rail to ensure the wish comes true. I read a few: a happy marriage; healthy children; peace; wealth. In the distance, I could see the cranes and cargo containers being stacked up from the cargo ships that pass through Singapore every day. To the left of that, an iconic modern structure—a set of apartment blocks that looks like shards of glass or ice forming out of the ground. Below me on the hillside of Mount Faber was thick rainforest, and then on the rail upon which I was leaning, the hopes and dreams of people for the future. It was a perfect, and perhaps, poetic cross-section of what I had experienced on my pilgrimage. Singapore—an industrious country set on a rainforest island, a world leader in modernity—building and showcasing cutting edge architecture all over the city. All these things are possible because of the dream of its people for the future and all of these things pave the way for what is to come.

The country also values family high on its list. The multiple playgrounds and the intentions behind them are clear proof of that. Anywhere you go on this island, you will hear Singaporeans calling older people *aunty* or *uncle*. Kids in those playgrounds refer to each other as *kor kor, jie jie, di di* or *mei mei*—meaning big brother, big sister, little brother, or little sister in Chinese. These traits of the playground show that from a young age, community is valuable and family, too, is valuable.

In 2014, Millie and I went to the top of Mount Faber and wrote our own wish on our own bell. Our wish was "A HAPPY FUTURE FOR OUR FAMILY." I'm not sure why I wrote on the bell in capitals—maybe I wanted to shout it! I don't think for one moment that our writing on a bell and hanging it from a railing on Mount Faber would secure this wish, but it does show me that we value happiness in our family. Valuing it, to us, isn't just talking about it, or even wishing for it. It is something we fight for when our kids are unkind to each other, it's what I remind myself after a long day at work and I don't feel like being a present and active parent. To me, a happy family is gold. It's gold for the children growing up in it and it's gold for the parents who try to steer it. Missing my wife and kids on this short pilgrimage—when I was tired and aching—showed me where my values lie and what is in my heart at its core. I was proud of the fact that it is something that my country of birth holds as valuable, too.

A pilgrimage is a journey that someone takes to a place unknown to them, in order to find something new about the land and about themselves. Perhaps I shouldn't limit my pilgrimage to a 74km hike, or even a 153.6km hike. Perhaps life is one long pilgrimage where we continue to learn about ourselves and the world. I don't feel like anything is missing, but I am really interested to see what I might find. Many of the thoughts and discoveries are brand new to me and, through this process, I am finding out an incredible amount about my country and about myself. I am very pleased to say that I like what I am finding and I wonder what else I might uncover on this journey.

Chapter 3

WONDERLUST

When I was a kid, my father had a giant camcorder. It was the height of technology—there were no smartphones to slide out of your pocket to snap and post onto Instagram or TikTok, but a huge, shoulder-mounted camera that took the shots on tape. It lived in a giant, grey plastic case which had fastening clips that made a loud "snap!" sound when my father opened them to film our family adventures. There were no clever transitions or cuts, just a start recording and stop recording function. Maybe a slow zoom, too. It didn't have a screen to watch your subject or to review your recordings, just an eyepiece to look through for real-time events. I remember my father allowing us to look through it, but we weren't allowed to press the red record button—film was valuable, the moment it had run out, you couldn't go back and choose which clip to delete—it was the whole video or none of it!

Every now and again on a weekend, my father would announce that we were going to have a family video night. I loved family video night. The bottom drawer of a dark wooden side-board in the living room contained all of our tapes. I can still hear the sound of the round brass-ring handles bouncing on the drawer after we pulled it open in anticipation. We would pull out the VHS-C cassettes, each one like a thicker version of an audio cassette (if you even know what those were!) and sift through the labels to see which video we would like to watch. Some of the labels had a previous holiday or afternoon walk tippexed off and the fresh title of the newly-recorded footage was written over it. I guess my father felt the previous footage wasn't interesting enough to keep. My sisters and I would take it in turns to put the cassette into the VHS adapter and I loved watching the mechanics automatically move the ribbon tape into place as a tiny motor buzzed, pushing everything into action— adding to the magic of the whole experience. We would wait in anticipation as we re-wound the videos to be able to watch from the beginning, and then, the show would start.

I loved reliving those memories and in my mind I was transported to a different time, like a trip to Australia when I was just two years old, running towards the sea, away from my heavily pregnant mother who frantically chased me while my father just giggled while filming. Watching the videos kept each past holiday fresh and current—the distant memories brought closer. I have a love-hate relationship with the video from our family holiday in Oban, Scotland. Despite being a bit older at the time, it is one that I remember only through the videos, rather than from memories. It was an amazing holiday, but it is also one of the most cringey videos you will ever see of three kids singing "Doe, a Deer" from the movie, *The Sound of Music*, complete with actions. Of course, that's the part I hate. I love the rest of it. The cottage in which we stayed was white. There was a tin bath in an old fashioned bathroom and an upstairs family room, with wooden floors, lined with a rug. We played badminton in the garden, which was behind the cottage and surrounded by thick forest. There was a little brook between the forest and the garden and I can remember the sound of the water making its way through the small rocks. Somehow, on camera, my dad managed to catch the damp-summer atmosphere that is unique to Scotland and which, as an adult, I have since experienced and enjoyed.

I loved the videos of our Sunday afternoon walks along the River Thames—my dad filmed a family of coots over a few consecutive weeks. I still have a mug with my name on it that my parents bought for me from a shop along the riverside. Each video showed the growth of the chicks into adults on their makeshift nest inside a floating old car tyre which bobbed up and down on the waves made by passing boats. I can just picture walking down the banks of the Thames, the sun beating down on us. I can even feel the atmosphere of the day, the way the sun warmed my back and the chills I felt when the clouds blocked its rays for a minute or two. I can hear the engines of the boats on the water and the crunch of the stony path under the feet of the people around us. We would walk through some public gardens—one of them had an aviary and I can still smell the dampness of the plants and hear the echo of our voices bouncing off the glass panels. I can see the view of the river and the water glistening in the sun, from a vantage point on Richmond Hill. I wonder whether the view has changed much since then.

There were a vast array of videos capturing my very cute little sister, who never failed to make us laugh, one way or another. In one of the videos, my sisters were on a see-saw. My mother was holding down the side upon which Amanda, my younger sister, was sitting. Charmaine, my older sister, was elevated on the other side. Assuming it was safe, my mother let go of the see-saw, sending my older sister to the ground and nearly launching Amanda into the air. Another time, we were on holiday in Somerset in the south of England and she had made friends with a little chick called Tinkerbell. For some reason Amanda had decided to rename it Annabel. I can hear the dialogue between my father and Amanda now.

"She's called Annabel," says Amanda, squatting over the poor chick, which was trying to walk away, but was being picked up and brought back by a chubby four year old with a bowl-shaped bob haircut.

"You mean, Tinkerbell?" replied my father.

"No, Annabel." There was a little resistance in her voice.

"Tinkerbell," came the calm response.

"Annabel!"

"It's Tinkerbell."

"Annabel!"

"So would you rather we called you Samanda?"

Amanda paused. You could almost see her processing the idea of the family changing her name. Then came the submission, "No, it's… Tinkerbell!" Oh, how we would laugh at these moments! In fact we still find it funny today.

We captured so many significant moments on the camcorder: our first experience of snow; my balloon bursting (a sad day!);

the blossom of Spring. None of these videos were given the chance to become nostalgic memories because they remained current by the videos and the experience of family video nights. I wonder whether my connection to Singapore was aided by these clips? We have an early clip from 1986—a family birthday, I think, of my great-grandma on my mother's side (we called her *Lao-Ma*). The whole family was there: aunties, uncles, cousins. We would pause the video and point out different cousins. "There's Jeremy and Shaun! … That one there is Elliott—oh, so cute!" I got to know my cousins through videos like this one and stories from my mother. I would miss them and wish I was part of the gang—this clan, my family—a long way away.

There seemed to be a lull in video or camcorder technology. One trip to Singapore, possibly around 2006, I borrowed my friend's camcorder. It was smaller than the one my father had—it still used tapes—but it recorded in high definition, and I think I filled six or seven tapes in total. I remember going over to Bintan Island in Indonesia for a few days that year. I filmed the crystal-clear waters one morning at around 7am. I must have been up late the night before because I fell asleep on the beach, completely zoned out. I woke, burnt to a crisp by the morning sun, and ran into the sea as I panicked, thinking my skin had blistered! I got away with just very red skin, which I tried to mask by wearing a bright red t-shirt. It probably just added to my radiant lobster vibe… Unfortunately, I didn't turn them into a video and I have no idea where those tapes are today.

When Millie and I began our own little family, we were fortunate to already live in the smartphone era. A year or two earlier, I remember getting back from our honeymoon in Rome and looking at our photos. There was a video in there from when I had accidentally chosen the wrong settings. It only lasted five seconds, and I was crossing a road while facing the Spanish Steps. It immediately brought me back. I could hear the traffic and voices, I could feel the atmosphere. So we started to take more videos. When Milo was born we began taking videos of him and a few of our little outings as a family. I had prior experience in video editing, having been taught by some really good content creators in my church, so I would collate a month's worth of videos into a five-minute roll and we would watch it back every now and again. Our first family holiday in Singapore in 2014 was a huge opportunity to take video—especially as we thought we may not return for a long time and by then, taking video instead of photos had become our habit.

As Milo and Aspen got a little older, I would declare family video night, just in the way my father did all those years ago. I would announce it as a reward, adding to the positive vibe of the family video night experience. "You have been so good lately that I think we'll have a family video night tonight!" The announcement was always met with a cheer. Just like when I was young, these long-passed events became recent memories in the minds and hearts of my own kids and I hope to continue family video night into double digits, teens and beyond—if they still enjoy them by then. One of their favourites is our day at Disneyland, Paris in the summer of 2017. Aspen had just turned two and Milo, six, and to be perfectly honest, we went there more for Millie and me to enjoy, rather than a day out for the kids. Our good friend Callum came with us, too—for a big two-week road trip around France and Spain actually, and this day was the culmination. Despite their young ages, both Milo and Aspen remember it like it was yesterday, the memory kept alive by recent viewings of the video.

When we knew we were moving to Singapore, we started to show some of our family videos of previous holidays to our close friends—the ones who wanted to come and visit us. We were so excited about moving, that I'm sure some of them were sick of our old videos, but they were always too polite to refuse them! It was such a great way of connecting them with Singapore life and culture and gave our friends a bit of insight into what we were looking forward to.

These opportunities to show friends and family our past videos and the memories of family video night gave us the idea to share our pending Singapore adventure with our friends and family via YouTube. We wanted our videos to be real—so we didn't go with the stereotypical YouTuber-influencer vibe, but a *this-is-how-we-are-really-doing* sort of vibe, which would accurately reflect our experiences, the highs and lows of relocation and the reality of family dynamics in a new country. I hoped that when my friends and family received a notification that we had uploaded a new video, they would perhaps share a bit of the excitement I used to have, watching those old family videos as a kid.

We decided to repurpose a YouTube page of ours that had about 15 subscribers, which was called *Finders Keepers*. I had started a travel blog a few years before under that name and the idea was that as we found beautiful moments, we could keep them forever as memories: finders keepers. As with many fads, content creation slowed to a halt and I had lost all momentum with it, totalling only four videos. With the blessing of time during the first UK COVID-19 lockdown that started in March 2020, Millie and I decided we would commit to making a video a week to keep our friends and family up-to-date with how things were going with us in the lead-up to our move abroad. And so in May 2020, we began making weekly YouTube videos.

Having moved to Surrey in the south of England only two years before, we realised that many of our new friends would have no idea why we had chosen Singapore as our future home and so we decided our first episode would be titled, *Why Singapore?* We sat down at the dining table, propped up my phone on a stack of books and started to talk. It was a sunny day. We faced the big glass doors that opened out to our garden where the kids were playing and kept an eye on them, as we had no idea how long the process would take. Thirty minutes later, we had a video! I loaded it into my laptop and began to edit. We mentioned a few of our past experiences in Singapore, so I grabbed some old photos and videos from our "Family Videos" hard drive (our modern-day version of the drawer full of tapes we had as kids) and put them into the video, too. We watched it over a few times and made a few tweaks.

For some reason, neither Millie nor I were that happy with the name, *Finders Keepers,* but neither of us said anything, not until after we had uploaded it to YouTube and scheduled it for release the next day. The change of name to WONDERLUST was very last minute, which involved us taking the video off

YouTube, and re-editing it with WONDERLUST at the start instead of *Finders Keepers,* and changing the channel name. WONDERLUST, deliberately spelled with an O (not wanderlust), was a made-up verb: to long for, search out, and lust after the wonder of the world. We were very aware that relocation, while it includes adventure, excitement and even a level of glamour, has its very real, difficult and trying times. We were not naive enough to think that our move was going to be perfect and so this channel name would be a weekly reminder to us to look for the extraordinary wonders in our ordinary lives; the idea that wonderful things are out there, we just need to look for them, even when the going gets tough.

We deleted the old videos from the channel to create a blank canvas and after about a week, our first video hit 100 views. We were surprised but very happy that 100 people would want to keep up to date with us! We created a second video and released it on time. Our commitment was holding strong—well, two weeks strong was good for us on this video creation thing. Then came that call, telling me that I no longer had a job due to the COVID-19 fallout in the international school scene in Singapore.

We had made a commitment to weekly videos and, to be honest, I really didn't want to keep going, but we felt it was important, especially as many friends were excited for our move and were expecting us to fly out in little over a month. So we stuck to our commitment and planned to tell everyone via our channel that the job had gone. We recorded our feelings over the week. I guess for me, it helped to add a bit of stability in a very unstable situation. The afternoon of the call, I remember taking out my phone, hitting record and no words came out of my mount. I just looked into the camera, saying nothing… for a very long time. It felt like minutes. Not knowing what to say, not knowing what I was feeling. The next day, I was feeling particularly low and Millie forced me to go out for a walk in a beautiful part of Guildford, near where we were living, called St. Catherine's Lock. We filmed and took photos. It was like therapy, finding the extraordinary wonder in our ordinary, and at the time, emotionally painful lives. I felt my spirit lifted as I was forced to look for the positives. I was glad we video-documented what we were feeling and what we were going through, emotionally. It has helped us to look back on it and be grateful for where we are now.

We stuck to our commitment, showing the lows and the highs of that week and then the build up to us leaving for Singapore. We never wanted to be YouTubers—YouTube was just the tool for sharing our journey with our friends and family. Over the weeks, I taught Millie how to edit videos and she learned very quickly, taking over the main running of the channel. We filmed our last few days and our departure. We landed in Singapore and filmed our Stay at Home Notice, or SHN, where the Singapore Government put incoming travellers into a two-week quarantine at a designated facility. We were so fortunate to stay in a five-star hotel and to have been given a suite—even after two weeks in one hotel room, we were able to remain motivated to video-document our stay. We filmed our first day of freedom and the things we got up to that week, eating and shopping along Orchard Road, Singapore's main shopping thoroughfare, where we stayed for our first week out of SHN. I think sharing our experiences of five-star quarantine was probably the first episode that interested viewers other than our friends and family.

Two weeks (and two YouTube episodes later) we received an email from YouTube, congratulating us on reaching our first 100 subscribers. We were very surprised that so many people would follow our journey and so we were encouraged to continue making our videos. Little did we know that this number in the following weeks would grow: 500, then 1000+ subscribers. We were absolutely shocked. A thousand people had subscribed to follow our little family and what we get up to in the week, and so our YouTube journey was started.

As my work as a teacher can be fairly time (and mentally!) consuming, we decided that Millie would take a lead role in content creation and video editing. She has blown me away with how quickly she learns techniques and applies what she has learned. She still gets a little panicky when the computer plays up, or when things are not gelling as well as she would like but, largely, she tackles each problem with composure and each glitch with determination. Through the channel and its Instagram account, she has loved being in touch with people— strangers from all walks of life and from all corners of the globe, who seem to be interested in our family. She has advised mums and shared wisdom on parenting. She has helped people who were considering relocation. She even arranges to meet people who have recently moved to Singapore to help them settle in and meet other people, too. I am so proud of the way she so gracefully and humbly uses her platform that the channel has given her to help people, to serve their needs and to share her wisdom.

* * *

In the months that followed the channel's initial rise in success, an increasing number of viewers asked about my heritage, or asked more questions about my background as a Singaporean-born Brit. There were many contrasting opinions about my return. Some felt I was a "returning son of Singapore" and others felt I had no place in returning home. Every time I explored my heritage, or felt a sense of belonging on an episode, it was met with comments of support (and very occasionally, resistance). As a result we felt that it would be a good chance to let our viewers in on the internal journey I was experiencing and so I took a camera along with me on that morning in Ang Mo Kio. I started to express the tension of feeling like I was home, despite not knowing much about my heritage, or even really that much about Singapore. I felt like a local, but at the same time, I also felt like an immigrant. I realised that morning that I could embrace both, and so the series title was born. Little did I know that morning, *The Local Immigrant* would also be a title I would embrace as me—not just a YouTube series.

To our surprise, many people were interested in my journey and all the more could relate. It seemed that this question of what makes Singapore "home" is one that resonated with many but was perhaps a question not often openly asked by Singaporeans or her residents. Questions about *heart, heritage* and *home* were being asked by so many more than just Singaporeans—I even heard from people in other parts of the world who felt the same way about their countries of birth. It has driven me to understand what it is that makes people feel at home and has led me to explore culture, heritage, upbringing and more.

At this time of writing, the WONDERLUST channel continues to grow in its reach. Millie had intended on studying again when we arrived here in Singapore, but she has found a new passion in creating videos. While the channel seems to have some momentum, she has put the formal studying on hold and is committed to creating more and better content. We still follow the original purpose of the channel, documenting our family's adventures, and being as real as we can. We share our bad days when things go wrong and, as parents, when kids have tricky periods. More than anything, we have remained committed to finding the extraordinary wonder in our ordinary lives. We hope it inspires our viewers to do the same.

Chapter 4

What Makes a Singaporean?

I could not deny that I felt Singaporean and I was beginning to be able to define what it was that was making me feel this way. There were many different contributing factors to my feeling of being home. I felt more comfortable and possibly even happier in warmer climates; our family dynamics were well-suited to an environment in which we could spend more time outdoors; having grown up with Singaporean food in my childhood home, the food culture in Singapore clearly suited me. Delicious food is available round the clock at affordable prices. I also really connect with the respect that Singaporeans show each other, particularly the older generations. But instead of simply accepting my feeling of belonging in Singapore, I wanted to examine it in more detail, to see whether I had nationalistic Singaporean traits and whether non-Singaporeans would identify me as Singaporean. So, I began to watch people. I analysed, questioned, anticipated, confirmed.

As new residents to Singapore, we were keen to make friends and had met some nice people and decided to host them and some of their friends too, for a dinner party at our place. There were three couples, two of whom had kids—but one set was at home with their helper and the other had babysitters looking after their kids. One couple were Singaporean, one couple were Malaysians who had lived in Singapore quite some years and the other couple were an even split—Malaysian wife and Singaporean husband. We didn't know any of them well, and it was the first time we were meeting one of the couples, but we were excited to host and make some new friends. Before living in Singapore, I had no idea how close the relationship between Singapore and Malaysia was—probably closer than brother and sister—perhaps more like twins separated at birth. Many Singaporeans have family from Malaysia, or have Malaysian heritage—just like me.

I was in the kitchen, cooking—western food, as we thought it would be a nice change of menu for our local friends. The first couple to arrive was the couple we had not met before. They came in and we introduced ourselves. Our kids were still awake, waiting up to meet our guests before they went to bed. I offered drinks to our guests and asked them to make themselves feel at home while I finished preparing our meal. I loved how they played with our kids—naturally, engaging with them, taking an interest. This is a trait I have noticed to be very common in Singaporeans. It is, to me, the *kampong* spirit that is still intertwined in Singaporean culture—one where everyone is welcomed as family and comfortable as family. The other couples arrived and each of them paid attention to our children like they were a niece and nephew. It was not awkward—familiarity with strangers.

Our kids said goodnight and went to sleep. Admittedly, it isn't normally that straightforward, but this was a good night! As

I made final preparations for dinner the others, with Millie, were standing around having a chat. They all knew each other already, but neither Millie nor I felt excluded by their conversation. We sat down to eat and the conversation turned to work. Work is something Singaporeans all seem to love talking about. One of the men worked as an engineer, managing a team of engineers who fixed huge cargo ships. Engines the size of large houses would break down in the middle of the ocean and he would have to deploy his team, all from his office in Singapore. Sometimes he'd be called in the middle of the night and he would have to wake himself up enough to solve the problem. Among the others were a lawyer and a doctor, an entrepreneur, an accountant and a stay-at-home mother (and part-time editor). Then there was me, a teacher and Millie, a YouTuber.

Conversation began to flourish as we discussed how many people or teams each person managed and strangely, I felt myself needing to put forward my credentials as a Head of Department and to talk about my responsibilities in organising schedules and maintaining strong relationships with my team, as well as setting goals and working towards success. Each person around the table appeared to grow in confidence as they spoke about work. Subtle hints to previous responsibilities and professional experiences were dropped in, I felt, to further validate themselves. Please don't get me wrong. These were good people—I mean, really good people. They care. They are real. They love. They are not pretentious and they are not arrogant. Kind people. I am not depicting our evening as a negative experience—in fact, we had a great time and would happily do it again with the same people!

But in my habit of analysis, I was suddenly aware that I was looking for value in what I did, not in who I was. I consciously held back from saying more on those lines and redirected conversation towards how much there was to enjoy in Singapore. To my surprise, Millie and I appeared to have seen much more of the country in our short six months, in comparison to locals who had lived here many years.

I have noticed that Singaporeans truly are hard workers. It seems to be the land of start-ups and networking. Everyone knows someone and everyone is fighting to be successful. It goes beyond the materialistic pursuits that I see in the UK. For us and many of our friends in the UK, to be financially stable was about being comfortable, about owning a house or having nice things. In Singapore there is a different emphasis. Some of it is pride— showing pride in our nation and also pride in ourselves. Hard work is valued and there is a culture of being successful. From the strong work ethic I get the impression everyone feels the need to contribute to society. Perhaps this is a necessity—there are no handouts in Singapore. In the UK, if you can't work, there are government benefits and the range of benefits are wide, and so for some, the desire to work and be successful isn't part of their mindset. I guess there isn't really that choice in Singapore.

The jobs and lives of the friends we hosted and the conversations we had with them may not be particularly surprising. Singapore is an incredibly industrious country. It has developed at an astonishing speed and is now a world leader in both building a dynamic city as well as conserving wildlife. In order to have been able to develop this status and well-deserved reputation, Singapore has had to adopt a hard-working culture. I have noticed there is a mindset that one needs to be busy in Singapore. It seems to be an unspoken rule that you are not allowed to say you are relaxing, or that you have time on your hands. When local friends tell me they are feeling chilled, or that their week has not been busy (I think it has happened twice in total), I have been really surprised. Ask a Singaporean how their week has been and the answer will be "busy" or "stressful", even if it is not necessarily true.

I have been trying to make a deliberate point to enjoy the spaces in my week—the 20 minutes I have to myself between when I get home and dinner time; my dinner times with Millie and the kids; our Netflix time after the kids go to bed. I want these to be the focus of my week when people ask me how it's going. I do feel under pressure, or concerned that sometimes people may feel like I am a bum, or that my job is easy—it really isn't—but perception is so often the truth for people and I have decided that I need to look at the space in time I have. I'm not trying to counter Singapore's culture, but the constant perception of being busy and stressed as a target is not healthy and I don't want to fall into that trap. Also, perhaps my friends and the people I meet will be led to believe (correctly) that I always have time for them and that it is never a hassle to ask me for help. I like that thought.

***

Orchard Road is Singapore's main shopping district. Its reputation sits high alongside London's Oxford Street and the Champs-Élysées of Paris and so there's no surprise that Orchard

Road is adorned with high-end stores. Louis Vuitton has even landed two prominent spots along the road. The shadows cast by the 28 shopping centres along the pavements used to be the shadows of trees from the nutmeg orchards that gave the road its name. People overflow from the air-conditioned malls onto the streets: some amble along, whereas others seem to race.

As part of our YouTube series, I decided that it would be interesting to test public opinion on the traits of Singaporeans. Orchard Road was a good contrast to the heartlands of Ang Mo Kio, where we filmed the first episode and so I took to the streets with a camera and a set of questions to see if I could discover more about Singaporeans—and more about myself.

The first thing I learned was that Singaporeans were surprisingly shy. They hid away from the camera, and some were even reluctant to stop. I asked about 35 people, or groups of people, and only four stopped. This surprised me. The dinner we hosted had no shortage of conversation, thought or opinion, and so I had set out with the expectation that the same would apply with the general public on the streets. I have come to learn that a camera and the potential of being shown on a screen can be very daunting to most Singaporeans.

"Hello, are you Singaporean?" was my opening line—I was keen to get the thoughts of Singapore's own people. People suddenly changed direction, or put their heads down, looking at the floor. Denied. "Good morning, are you Singaporeans by any chance?" A stare into a phone, a dismissive wave. Denied again. Of those who responded, most people were not Singaporeans but Indonesian, Malaysian, Chinese, Thai and Indian.

And then occasionally, "Yes, I am!"

"Great! My name is Jonty Tan, I am working on a project to find out what makes a Singaporean a Singaporean and I was hoping you wouldn't mind answering a few questions on camera?" I was enthusiastic, as polite as I could be... with my clearly British in accent. Perhaps I sounded too official.

"I'm afraid not, sorry." No explanations, just rejection.

Eventually, I caught the eye of a group of three lads, probably in their early- to mid-20s. They saw I had a couple of cameras and looked curious. "I wondered if you would be happy to answer a few questions on camera?" They were! Interestingly, one of the lads had just been sworn in as a citizen of Singapore and his two friends were born and bred Singaporeans. They were well-turned out and spoke confidently. Some of their observations were more about the style and fashion of young Singaporeans.

I managed to catch a fairly broad cross-section of Singapore's society in the four groups of people who stopped to talk with me. After those lads, an Indian Singaporean in his 30s stopped to speak with me. He was particularly proud that, in his opinion, Singaporeans see "human—not colour or race". He explained that Singaporeans had become better at putting others first—giving the example of giving space to a wheelchair user at the front of the line for an elevator, although he expressed his frustration that some people will still cut in front of wheelchair users and parents with pushchairs to get to their destination quickly. A couple in their late-20s of Chinese heritage stopped to talk, too. At the last minute, the man decided he was too shy for the camera and left his partner to do the talking. She was articulate and clear in her thoughts and opinions. Finally, I spoke with a married couple who were Peranakan and Cantonese. They were in their early seventies and had clear ideas on the traits of Singaporeans. I found it interesting as they described heritage as "what we see around us... we used to be a small fishing village and now, we are a bustling metropolis". I liked that they were proud of what the country had become, despite its drastic and rapid modernisation. Each of these differing opinions shed a different hue of light onto my thoughts on what makes a Singaporean and I was pleased to hear this wide spread of ages and races speak so positively about Singapore.

This married couple also mentioned *kiasu-ism*—the fear of losing out, or "scared to lose". This can be seen in parents who fervently send their children to further tuition after school to ensure their grades are at the top of the class. The group of lads I spoke with first mentioned joining a queue at the fear of missing out on the latest trend or good food. This trait is intertwined with every attitude and idea and is probably one of the key factors in Singapore's success.

In a small way, I could see *kiasu-ism* growing in me! I take the MRT to work and have to change lines at a fairly busy station. The race for first place to the escalators starts on the train, half way between the previous stop and the interchange. Commuters stand and make their way to the train doors, standing close enough to mark their territory. Having only one stop before the interchange, I tend to stand near the doors. Occasionally, someone will stand in the two-foot gap between me and the exit, breathing into the window like a enraged bull. Sometimes, someone else will squeeze in next to me, placing their foot just in front of mine. All of a sudden the train halts and the doors open. Like horses out of the gates, there's a mad dash—walking, so as not to give away how desperate we all are to get there first. I know this is a race to the escalator, and not a hurry to work, as the moment the commuters get to the escalator they stand there, instead of walking up (this is usually when I walk up, overtaking everyone who beat me to the escalator!). Perhaps there is a *kiasu* Singaporean in me!

***

Over the past couple of years, I have heard many differing opinions regarding Singapore's government and culture. These opinions range from very positive, patriotic comments to the angry and negative. I am not a politician and do not aim to discuss policies or parties, but I think there is value in sharing my thoughts and observations of people I have met towards the government, as these observations are relevant to my journey of discovery. I have begun to see a pattern, or at least trends, regarding these wildly differing opinions, and have noticed two clear factors in the divisions of opinions that I have heard.

The first is a generational factor. Singapore is fantastic at honouring the generations that have contributed most to the development of the country. One group is the pioneer and Merdeka generations. The pioneers are my grandparents' generation, those who were involved in the foundation of Singapore. They dreamt of what Singapore could be and worked towards it. They made sacrifices to transform Singapore into what it is today and they remember what Singapore was like in its early days—some, like my grandparents, even remember what it was like living under the Japanese occupation in World War II. These people are largely positive about the country and what it has become, knowing by experience as well as contribution, Singapore's growth in strength.

The Merdeka generation are the people who had childhoods in the 1950s and 60s—my parents are part of this generation. They helped to lay a firm foundation for Singapore. I have noticed this generation is still very much aware of how far Singapore has come. They have seen the improvements in the country over their lifetime and value their principles of hard work and determination. They, too, experienced Singapore in its early days, some growing up in *kampongs* and now living in high rise apartments.

These experiences of the past I think give a greater context and I do wonder whether Singapore's rapid modernisation and constant updating may contribute to a lesser understanding of this context for the younger generations. While there are many fantastic museums across the country, they are just that— museums. In Europe we grow up with a living history. Old buildings and monuments are everywhere, all contributing to the education of the people of what has come before. I am aware that it is an excessive sense of history that may contribute to the British struggle to define who they are today, but perhaps a balance of both is needed. My grandpa would regularly share stories of life during the Japanese occupation in Singapore, and this led me to search out places like the Changi Chapel and Museum. There, the interactive displays and accounts that were presented brought to life what my grandparents and their generation lived through. It is such a contrast to what Singapore looks like today. To call it a contrast is an understatement—it is otherworldly.

My generation and younger seem to be divided in their opinions and the trends are often based on whether the individuals have travelled or lived abroad or not. I had a conversation a few weeks ago with someone who was angry that the government would force everyone to wear a mask during the COVID-19 pandemic. He explained that freedom of speech, to him, was a myth in Singapore and that if he protested by taking off his mask, he would be fined and imprisoned. I tried to explain to him the alternative—my friends and family in the UK had spent the past 12 months in their homes, unable to see each other, unable to go out, with thousands dying from this horrendous virus. In July 2020, hundreds of people filled London's Hyde Park to use their freedom of speech to protest the wearing of masks. Some even wore masks, with the mouth and nose areas cut out. I do understand why there is a desire to be able to freely express, but at the same time, I am deeply concerned about the selfishness expressed at the expense of other people's lives. By the end of 2021, there had been close to 150,000 deaths in the UK alone due to COVID-19.

Those who have lived abroad have seen the impact of "freedom" in other countries and what happens without a strong sense of responsibility. These Singaporeans are largely happy with the way the government runs things and are incredibly appreciative of living in a safe country with strict penalties for law breakers. Singapore's consequences of high fines, imprisonment and corporal punishment may seem harsh, but they clearly highlight what is, and what is not, acceptable behaviour for a kind, safe and respectful society. Singapore's reputation of being a safe place to live and bring up children is an accurate one. We feel safe to let our kids go and buy a drink from the stall at the hawker centre. We know that if we leave our phone or wallet out on a table or on a bench in a public place, it is more than likely going to find its way back into our hands. Some would argue that these things are not stolen because of fear of consequences, but I see it as a firm deterrent, a clear boundary to teach respect for personal property. I believe these strict laws have taught Singaporeans to value people's property. Of course, these laws are not limited to property, but also the way Singaporeans respect others. By valuing someone's possessions you in turn value *them*.

These strict laws that promote respect are perhaps a large contributor to one of the opinions I heard on Orchard Road that day. The guy in his 30s felt strongly that Singaporeans "do not see race, they see *human*." While Singapore is by no means an ideal society, it is getting a lot right. There is still room for improvement. There is, from what I can see, a racial hierarchy within the harmony, those with Chinese heritage having the upper hand. I guess it makes sense for there to be a greater influence from China, since approximately 75 per cent of Singaporeans are of ethnic Chinese heritage. China is the local superpower and the second largest economy on the planet.

Since the 1990s, China has lifted more than 750 million people out of poverty—the country often gets a bad press in the West, but they are doing a lot of good. What doesn't make sense to me—and this is a global issue—is how people can continue to treat other people negatively because of the colour of their skin and their heritage. In Singapore we have a National Pledge which is declared every year by the whole nation on National Day. It addresses this inequal treatment of people and sets out the aim, which is:

"We, the citizens of Singapore,
pledge ourselves as one united people,
regardless of race, language or religion,
to build a democratic society
based on justice and equality
so as to achieve happiness, prosperity
and progress for our nation."

This pledge, learned and recited by schoolchildren every day, places a priority on unity as a nation and I can see it. There is harmony. There is a huge amount of respect. This is something laid into the very foundations of Singapore. It is not perfect—Singapore is not a utopia, but its aims are clear and while it may never reach full harmony, setting it out as a constant goal is healthy. I think of our founding Prime Minister, Mr Lee Kuan Yew, who in 1966 said:

"Eventually, what happens in the long run depends upon how we solve our problems here. And the best way to ensure our survival and to ensure an enduring future is through a multi-racial society. By that I mean a society which is tolerant to all groups, which gives a chance to everybody."

In 1989 the Ethic Integration Policy was introduced, a required quota of different races on each floor of high-rise HDB apartment blocks—promoting the racial harmony set out by the Prime Minister. Even today, if you were to walk along the corridors of an HDB apartment block at around 6pm, you could begin to smell the varied blend of flavours—Indian spices, Chinese dishes, Malay aromas, all mixing in the air. It is a unique and special feature of Singapore.

***

Interestingly to me, all of the people with whom I spoke on the sidewalks of Orchard Road were consistent in identifying one main trait of a Singaporean: a Singaporean speaks Singlish. My interviewees told me that they could go to any country in the world and immediately identify a Singaporean by their use of Singlish. Can I speak Singlish? Not really, no. I can kind of put on a Singaporean accent and use the odd Malay word here and there, but in my experience, what makes Singlish so unique is that it isn't a taught language. It's a caught language. Its tonal flow and use of Malay, Cantonese, Hokkien, Teochew, Mandarin and Tamil almost create a dialect of its own. These many different languages represented in Singlish reflect the melting pot of cultures that is Singapore. This is what makes it unique to this tiny country. Each phrase or word in Singlish has a reason and a story behind why it is used. Each word, therefore, is intertwined with the building blocks of Singapore and so I can understand why it is seen as a defining feature of a Singaporean.

The problem with Singlish being *caught,* rather than *taught,* is that I can't get lessons in Singlish. These are phrases I need to pick up and absorb from the people around me. And the problem there is that I work in an international school and even my local friends try to meet me in the middle, by talking a little clearer and less "local" when they are with me! So it may be a slow journey.

As you could imagine, this understanding of how important the use of Singlish is in making a Singaporean was a fairly disappointing pot hole in my road of discovery. I do not have the one main feature of a Singaporean. But I still felt I belonged in Singapore, and there was an undeniable sense of belonging that I had. Perhaps my surface seems more anglicised—I have a very English accent and apparently I dress like a Brit and walk like one, too (whatever a British walk is!). But beneath the surface is someone who belongs on the tiny red dot. I guess, in time, I will pick up some Singlish phrases. I mean, my accent already changes when I speak to hawker stall owners or taxi drivers— so it's only a matter of time, right? The only issue with this is that I feel Singaporean *now.* What is it that gives me this sense of belonging? Why do I connect so tightly to the culture?

Chapter 5

Lost Identity

Britain, for all its history and depth of heritage and culture, appears to be losing its sense of identity. It may already be lost. In 2011, the British government's Department for Education introduced British values into the primary school curriculum. I was teaching in a state school at the time—a government funded school, free for students to attend. These are the norm in England, with only six per cent of children going to independent schools. My school was a newer building, but it managed to maintain the atmosphere of a classic British primary school. The uniform was a polo t-shirt and a sweater and the students wore grey trousers or skirts. In the warmer months, the girls wore gingham summer dresses. Each classroom had a big rug near the front where the students would sit during registration or during some lessons or story time. Colourful displays littered the walls, showcasing student work. The children would be so proud if their work made it onto the display. The staffroom was purpose built, with space for all teachers to sit and meet. It was built with big glass walls facing the open atrium, which was filled with daylight from the floor to ceiling windows. Students used to walk past the room when meetings were going on and most of them would stare intensely at the floor, avoiding looking up at all costs—but every now and again one would try to look in. We'd even get some kids who would pull faces and then immediately regret it.

I remember the discussions in the staffroom when we were told about teaching British values. The British teachers were finding it hard to identify what those values were. This isn't to say British people have no values—they definitely do, but my colleagues and I found it hard to identify what made those values uniquely British, rather than human. The government landed on five values: democracy, the rule of law, individual liberty, mutual respect and tolerance of those with different faiths and beliefs. While I understand and agree that these are all good values to have, I wouldn't say they were exclusively British, and to teach them in school as "British" made me sometimes feel like we were saying these simple, formative values for any working society were, by dis-association, not the way everyone else lived.

It felt that for many of the British public, the Brexit vote was based on an identity crisis. Many of the pro-Brexiteers were reaching for something they felt had been lost: Britishness. Britain over the years has expanded its territory into much of the world—at its height, the British Empire covered a whopping 24 per cent of the world, including Singapore. There are remnants of the empire all over Singapore: buildings like Raffles Hotel and the black-and-white mock Tudor houses are among the most iconic and sought after.

Recently, soul-searching about identity has been happening

across the globe, and Britain is no exception. Many Brits are standing up against racism, standing strongly for human rights. But by doing so, they also need to redefine what is British. After all, Britain was built upon colonisation, discovering lands that were already inhabited and claiming it as their own. It was the English who sailed to America and named the natives "Indian" because of the colour of their skin. It would be a travesty today if anyone did the same, and it was very much a different age back then. But ancestry is intertwined with one's identity and so it is important for the British people to find their values, the things they are proud of and the elements that help to define them as a country.

**

For me, there is so much that Britain should celebrate as its heritage and cultural identity. I have taught in both state and private schools in England, as well as started my schooling in a state school before moving into the private system. I went to an all-boys independent school—Whitgift School—on the outskirts of Croydon in Surrey in the south of England. It was, and still is, known as one of the best schools the British system has to offer and had a reputation for breeding rugby players, army officers, top musicians and influential businessmen. Recently, the England Rugby Union national team has fielded three players who all hailed from Whitgift, which has a history spanning over 400 years. Whitgift provided me with a very British education. The rich history of the school meant that some of our classroom desks still had lids that opened to reveal a space in which we could keep our books, as well as a space for inkwells. We were expected to use fountain pens—no ballpoints were allowed, and as a left-hander, I had to always be equipped with blotting paper to prevent my work from smudging. We even had strict hairstyle rules, not too short and not too long. Some students who had haircuts that were deemed too short were asked to stay at home until it was longer and I even remember a particularly hairy peer of mine being sent home at age 13 to have a shave.

My physics teacher was a very well-dressed, slim man called Dr. Shaw, who was bald and wore fashionable glasses. He played the double bass very well and claimed to be able to fit this instrument into his Audi TT, provided he opened the glovebox. I really enjoyed his lessons. One day, he must have been running late for our lesson as we were in the physics lab unsupervised. My friend and I were throwing around his pencil case, getting slightly out of hand. I kicked it hard and it went flying through the air, hitting a huge metal radiator. Little did I know, my friend had a solid, glass bottle of Quink Ink, which smashed and sprayed across the wall. I remember trying to take an ink eradicator pen to it, in some vain hope it would clear the mess, which it didn't.

We had a Combined Cadet Force, or CCF, which would gather on parade after school on Tuesdays. We represented the wide range of the armed forces, the Army, Navy and Royal Air Force. There was even a Corps of Drums. I chose the Army. I remember being very nervous. Some of the boys in my year group had these high-grade army boots, laced half way up their calves. My boots were ankle height and I had to wrap puttees from my ankles to my knees. Puttees were used by the British Army from before the Great War until the late 1930s, and for some reason we still used them in our school CCF! They were makeshift gaiters, used to keep baggy trouser legs tight so you didn't get snagged on anything and to stop stones falling into your boots. I didn't have a clue what they were for, or how I was supposed to wear them and I made some sort of attempt to copy the kids around me. I had no idea how they knew what to do. We had to wear these itchy, uncomfortable ribbed woollen jumpers and a woollen beret. I felt uncomfortable in the whole get-up. As an adult, I look back and think I would love the experience now. We had a rifle range at our school and we had the opportunity to shoot guns. We learned to march, we learned tactics and we learned hand signals in combat.

Some of the older boys were given the responsibility of NCO—non-commissioned officer. Part of their duties while we were on Army Camp were to ensure we slept at a good time and didn't make too much noise. They were always high on the power of their title and would yell at us and treat us unreasonably. We'd be made to do press-ups and run laps if they weren't keen on us. For some reason we were a bit scared of them and always did what they said. One year on Army Camp, our dormitory was all awake long after the lights-out curfew. We suddenly noticed that one of our peers had fallen asleep—*really* asleep. I can't remember who organised it, but six of us got around his bed and slowly picked up his mattress with him on it and walked him out into the cold stone corridor, where we left him. We had to do it as quietly as possible, without laughing, otherwise the NCOs would emerge and we'd be in a lot of trouble. It must have been winter as he woke up, shivering. Another night, a different kid fell asleep and we managed to build a tower of tables and chairs over him, so if he woke up startled, the whole thing would come crashing down. The NCOs caught us that time and we were all given a good rollicking, even our friend who was innocently asleep!

As a musician, I sometimes wonder whether I would have particularly enjoyed the Corps of Drums more than the army, but I don't think I was too fussed about the regalia and marching in fancy formation, despite really enjoying watching it in action. When I was a kid, on one of our holidays to Scotland, my dad took us to the Edinburgh Tattoo, which was held in the grounds of Edinburgh Castle—a majestic landmark on a hill in the heart of Edinburgh city. A tattoo in this context is a display of military music playing. The name, I think, comes from a Dutch phrase that was used to describe the time to close taverns. Military drummers would play to signal the end of the night, I guess, like a last-orders bell in the UK pubs. The drum corps would march in creative lines, creating patterns, and I remember willing them to bump arms or drums as they marched close to each other. One group threw drumsticks high into the air and then caught them again with absolute precision. Towards the end of the evening the sound of Scotland—the bagpipes—filled the air as kilted men played to another drum corps. I was only young, but the whole experience was one that has stayed with me and that I'll never forget.

It was a very good CCF and at times I would imagine I was experiencing what my dad did during his National Service, although I doubt it was anything close. A few of my friends ended up with scholarships to the Army, Navy and RAF, some becoming Army majors, and I understand the Ministry of Defence now sponsors the programme at the school.

The school fees were incredibly expensive, and I was fortunate that my music scholarship gave my parents a fee reduction. My mum also took on a new job in a high street bank to help pay for my education. I am more grateful than she'll ever really know—even though, at the time, I placed no value on how much things cost. Our school orchestra was of a high standard and by the time I was 18, I had performed in London's most iconic concert halls—The Royal Albert Hall, The Royal Festival Hall and Westminster Central Hall. I also enjoyed trips around the world, including a rugby tour to Prague in the Czech Republic and an orchestra tour to Japan. I regret not taking more pictures and journaling the trip as I remember very little of the sights. Most of my memories are from the few photos I did take. I was miles away from home and we had the company of some musicians from our all-girls sister school. The experience of being away from home with a group of girls was far more exciting than the adventure of being in a new land, although I remember some key moments and lessons about Japanese culture.

I celebrated my 17th birthday during that tour. Some friends and I went to a restaurant for dinner—a local restaurant, serving Japanese cuisine. We were asked to remove our shoes and there was a neat rack of slippers in the hallway before we went through to our dining area. We swapped our shoes for the slippers and made our way through. We sat on the floor and my mind's eye can see white cushions surrounding a dark wooden, square table, which was a comfortable distance from the ground for sitting and eating. My school friend, Mark, a clarinettist in the orchestra, had been learning Japanese at school and so he took care of the ordering. The food came and we tucked in, enjoying conversation and the company of three of our female musician friends. During our meal we saw a line for the washroom had formed and I remember joking with our table about it, suggesting that the various dishes we had ordered were the cause. We continued our meal and the line grew. I'm sure in my mind, the length of this line has elongated over time, providing a far more comical image, but I recall seven or eight uncomfortable looking customers, waiting for the washroom! Over the course of the evening we had been served by some friendly waitresses and so we were surprised when a more official-looking manager came to speak with us. "I'm sorry, but I think you are wearing all of the toilet slippers!" The restaurant (like much of Japan) had assigned slippers for people to wear when using the toilet and the line of customers had assumed they were all in use!

In my final year at school, I was awarded the responsibility of becoming a prefect—a senior student with authority and responsibilities. I was given a special tie to wear and during formal occasions I would be given a royal purple robe to wear. Looking back on it, I realise how pompous it all sounds, and how pompous it makes me feel, realising that all of this was perfectly normal to me at the time. Our headmaster would regularly entertain guests of honour, and as a music scholar, I would have to play my 'cello as part of a trio, quartet or quintet for them, which included Sir David Attenborough and even Queen Elizabeth II.

***

My very British schooling must have left a strong impression on me. I felt embraced by Britain, even adopted by her. Having spent 34 years in Britain, and having a very British schooling experience, I was keen to identify what British traits I have or which British values I hold, and to understand why, despite this, I feel more Singaporean than British. It was a much harder exercise than I initially thought. Britain, once an empire that ruled nearly a quarter of the world's land, steeped in history and heritage, now seemed to be questioning its identity. Has British culture really been whittled down to just afternoon tea and fish and chips?

Britain and its values are steeped in the church and so there's no surprise that some of the traditions I have come to love are associated with the Anglican Church. Millie and I were married in a beautiful church, set in the middle of nowhere in the countryside, near a farm and a large manor house. In the summertime, the surrounding fields would have different crops growing in them—barley, maize and sugarbeet—on rotation year on year. Our wedding day was freezing cold—it snowed that morning. We sent out text messages to all of our guests advising them to bring blankets and to wear wellington boots! Despite this, many still wore high heels and small skirts—and they suffered the cold as a result! Heels got stuck in the mud and legs went blue in the cold.

We honeymooned in Rome—a most unique and romantic city, which, in the middle of December, felt like it was exclusively ours. We arrived back in time for Christmas and spent it with my parents at their home in the east of England, near where we got married. We found out that the priest who conducted our wedding ran a midnight mass each Christmas Eve. The mass started at about 11pm and saw us through into Christmas Day. This became an annual visit as we spent more Christmases in the converted barn, which was, and still is, my parents' home. I love the tradition of midnight mass and will always try to attend one when in the UK for Christmas. I had attended a few midnight masses when I was younger and in my late teens and early 20s, my own version of midnight mass was a trip to the pub with friends for some Christmas Eve beers and wine. I remember one year, before smoking was banned indoors, we went to a pub in Croydon, then headed to a church for 11pm, stinking of cigarettes and alcohol. I'm not sure what the parishioners thought of us but I didn't feel like they were unhappy with our presence. We left shortly after midnight and went back to the pub.

Perhaps it is my faith, rekindled in my 20s, that makes me feel like Brits ought to find pride and joy in their traditional church services. While the church I am a part of is more modern, there's something about the old stone buildings, singing hymns that have been sung for centuries and the community of people taking a moment to celebrate something together that is a reflection of British-ness. Even now as I write this in tropical

Singapore, I think of Christmas carol services, candles glowing as choristers carry them to their stalls. As the Director of Music at a couple of independent schools over the past years, I have loved carol services and the sound of the choir resonating through a church. Those beautiful old buildings—I love their stone floors that have grooves worn out from where people have walked for centuries. I think also of the annual 11 November Remembrance Day services where countless representatives of the armed forces are honoured, remembering those who sacrificed so much to bring about peace in the nation and the world. I can just see congregations of people adorned with their poppies, that show the British spirit, the determination to grow and flourish, even in hard times.

Every now and again in Britain, the debate about the monarchy and its validity appears in the newspapers and then social media rolls out opinion after opinion, some of them hateful. I think the Monarchy gives Brits something proud to hold on to. It is one of, if not the oldest Monarchy on the planet.

The British countryside is peppered with historical monuments, houses, palaces and castles that speak of this heritage. In England, my family would visit Blickling Hall in Norfolk. It was the home of Anne Boleyn, one of King Henry VIII's wives, where she was born in 1507. It has beautiful, well-manicured gardens and beautifully preserved furniture. I proposed to Millie in the woodland grounds, next to the huge lake, in January 2011. It was a cold day and the sun was going down. I got down on one knee in the mud. I'm grateful she said "yes".

***

Brits love to talk about the weather: it's a defining trait of the British. I have come to notice that it is also a defining trait of Singaporeans, too! While the main feature of the discussion is largely contrasting (always too cold in Britain as opposed to always too hot in Singapore), there is one feature that connects the two: the rain. In Singapore, the rain comes down like a power-shower. Step out onto the street when it is raining, and you might as well have jumped into a river. There have been many occasions where I have been soaked to my underpants in Singapore. I don't tend to carry around an umbrella, contrary to most of the local advice. I think I quite like the novelty of warm rain. Perhaps that will change in time. In Britain, the rain is cold. If you get caught out in the rain, you will probably end up in a shiver. In fact, there have been many times I have been soaked to my underpants in Britain, too! But it's different, you can feel the cold rain running down your back. There is, however, one great thing about getting caught in the cold rain: warming up. There is something wonderful about soaking in a hot bathtub or under a warm shower after being cold and wet to the bone. I could soak for what felt like hours, feeling my body slowly thawing out. For a few years, we had the privilege of living in my parents' home in the countryside in Norfolk. They had underfloor heating in the bathrooms and I loved the warmth on my toes when I got out of the bath. That home also had an open fire and I loved thawing out in front of it.

Despite the regular rain and cloud, I loved getting outdoors and enjoying all that Britain's countryside had to offer. It is probably the only thing I really miss about living in the UK. Before moving to Singapore, I had the chance to spend a week at Plas y Brenin, or the "Place of Kings", which sits lakeside in the heart of the Snowdonia National Park in North Wales. Once an inn that hosted Queen Victoria and Kings Edward VII, George V and Edward VIII, it is now a 'gold standard' training centre for outdoor activities. It is also the main centre in the UK for anyone wanting to train for more serious mountain climbing trips, including expeditions to Mount Everest. Its surroundings are staggering. Clouds cling to the tops of the mountains, the beauty of the peaks reflecting in the lakes, creating diamond horizons.

My week at Plas y Brenin was filled with some of my favourite outdoor activities. We canoed, climbed rocks and summited mountains. I tried a couple of new activities, too. The first was gorge walking, or canyoning as it is sometimes known. The area used to be a copper mine and there were remnants of industrial life all around. Old machinery had been abandoned, rusting in the ground. Nature had repossessed the land upon which a big, stone building once housed mining equipment. We went a bit further downstream where we harnessed up, popped helmets on and started our ascent. We stepped into the fast flowing, ice cold mountain water, feet feeling initially refreshed and then achingly cold within seconds. As adrenaline started to pump around my body from climbing up a rope next to a small but powerful four-metre waterfall, my toes began to warm up. We waded through deeper parts of the gorge, water reaching waist height. At points, our instructor, Chris, who had pre-set ropes, would direct us along the edges of the gorge, gripping small holds of rock as we shuffled higher up the downward-rushing water. At times, the current would almost drive my legs from underneath me.

As the gorge opened out, perhaps five or six metres wide, small caves began to appear in the walls of the gorge. We went in one on the left. Immediately the water around our feet became ice cold again, as the darkness of the cave forced us to rely on feeling the rock around us. My excitement for the whole experience overshadowed my uneasy feeling, and my nervous knots added to the sense of adventure. My group became silent and all we could hear was our feet pushing through the deep puddles, and the low sound of small waterfalls that had carved their way through the rock. The sound our feet made reminded me of my mum running my bath as a kid. She would shuffle the water side to side with her hands to create more bubbles for our wash. As we followed the cave to an opening, the deep, powerful sound of pounding water became louder. We followed the sound to the other side of the gorge, where there was a smaller opening to another cave. I had to duck to get into it and my plastic helmet scraped across the underside of the rock as I misjudged its height. This cave was much brighter than the last one, and much louder, too. As I walked, hunched to avoid another head bang, there was no doubt that I was going to encounter some sort of waterfall. What looked like a hole in the ceiling had been carved into the rock and smoothed over with thousands of years of water, eroding its path downward. I put my hand out to touch the water. The power of the rushing white water batted my hand away. I had to tense my arm and hand to be able to keep it in place to feel the force. Behind the waterfall, the cave was shallow, only a metre or two deeper. I stood there, in what felt like a small cupboard, pinned in by the water. The sound of the rushing water was hard to describe—so loud that I couldn't hear anything else, but not deafening or uncomfortable.

The other new activity I tried over that week in Snowdonia was coasteering. Jumping off cliffs into the sea, climbing up rocks and swimming around the cove—when I was a kid, my parents called it messing around and being unsafe! But some clever people decided that by wearing helmets and buoyancy aids, we could give it a name—coasteering—and it would become a recognised activity. I was impressed by the varied activities that were available in a place where I used to just enjoy camping and hiking.

When we lived in Norfolk, we were very close to the shores of the North Sea, where sandy beaches would stretch out for miles. Some days we would walk for what felt like hours across the wet sands before reaching the water's edge. The British seaside can be seen as iconic. Places like Brighton and Blackpool became popular resorts in the late 1800s, when Brits would flock to the seaside to enjoy the health benefits of swimming in the sea. Today, Brits continue to descend upon these destinations, enjoying the glory of the British summer.

When Millie and I first got married, we would pack a tent, some food and firewood and drive out to the coast. Many Norfolk beaches had huge sand dunes that loomed over the sand and sea. These doubled up as quite hefty wind blockers and so we would pitch our tent in one of the mini craters that were nestled between tufts of marram grass and light our fire. On cold nights we would scoop warm sand from near the flames and pour it over our feet as we sat, staring at the animated flames under a bright, star-lit night sky. Over the years we would return, with one child and then two. Our kids love going to the beach. Beaches are one of their happy places. They can sit and play in the sand and water for hours without a care in the world. I love looking out at the horizon. It's a leveller for me. I see the British summertime as the glorious Britain—the green hills, birds chirping, the warmth of the sun making everything glow—but there really is something special about the beaches. Everyone is happy at the beach.

We celebrated Aspen's second birthday on the beach. We had already established that it was one of her happy places and, being a June baby, we banked on the weather being good for an afternoon in the sun. That morning it was super gloomy and so as we packed our things for a short drive to the beach, we left out some essentials, assuming the weather would not have lent itself to getting wet. Cromer is a beautiful beach town on the Norfolk coast, with stunning views over the North Sea. High and stormy tides can bring pelting waves onto the overlooking pathways, and the water has even flooded its 120-year-old pier. Calm summer days show the blue sea in all its glory: waves lapping on the shore, casual surfers taking on calm waves and the hum of enjoyment all around. The predictability of the unpredictable British weather meant that we were playing on the sand in the bright, warm sunshine without change of clothes, towels, swimsuits or even flip flops! Cue Aspen, down to nappy and a back-to-front baseball cap, and Milo in his briefs and vest! A couple of their friends joined them in the only-appropriate-on-a-sunny-beach-day attire and the adults waded into the cold North Sea with jeans pulled up to our knees and sweaters, to ensure our bodies stayed warm! This is an example of a classic British beach day!

After some time playing in the sand and wading in and out of the sea, we walked up to enjoy more British seaside classics—fish and chips and a cone of Mr Whippy ice cream. I love that every British person loves to have fish and chips at the seaside. You can be at opposite ends of the social ladder, but all enjoy fish and chips out of a newspaper while gazing out at the horizon. Strangely, I've met quite a number of Brits who find it hard to accept that fish and chips is a large part of the perceived culture: "Britain is so much more than just fish and chips!" they'd say. I agree. But fish and chips is a *part* of British culture and it needs to be embraced. Maybe those who live in-land, away from the seas, are the ones who struggle to identify. I think that one of the reasons why Brits are finding it hard to identify who they are and what their culture is, is that it isn't just one thing. It is an array of many things. Many different parts make a complete body and it is important to embrace each part to create a healthy sense of identity.

Britain is its education system, both state and private. Britain is the smell of the classrooms, the displays that hang from the ceiling, the colourful tables in the primary schools, the noise of the playground. Britain is the old desks that lift up to reveal book storage. The country is inkwells, ties and robes. Britain is her school orchestras and her love for football, rugby and cricket. Britain is the creaky floorboards of old cottages, the neatly mowed lawns in front or behind houses. Britain is old country homes and Royal palaces, the chapters of history written into tapestries, preserved in old bedrooms in ancient castles. Britain is the monarchy and the Anglican church. Britain is the Sunday roast and Yorkshire puddings. Britain is high tea, and she is picnics in the park. Britain is her rolling hills, the mountains, the rivers, the beaches. Britain is the rainy gloomy days that you want to spend under a blanket in front of the BBC. Britain is open fires in the pubs. Britain is her glorious summer days and her colourful autumn walks. She is the daffodils in spring and the crisp winter mornings. Britain is her military—steeped in history, in wars and battles. She is her aid to other countries and the good she provides to the world. Britain is each of these things and all of these things. Britain *is* fish and chips.

I love all of these things that are British and I wish that more Brits embraced them as part of who they are. I cannot deny that my love for, pride of, and ownership of these elements of British culture mean I will never be fully Singaporean. I wholeheartedly love Britain. But I will never feel completely British. I understand this is a common dilemma in third-culture, or cross-cultural kids, and it is something I choose to embrace. My heart and home lies across two nations and two cultures, but I feel like I belong in one.

Chapter 6

Found Heritage

In my journey to identify why I feel like a Singaporean I have been able to discover lots about my heritage. I have learned about the customs of my ancestors, where they have come from and a little about their journey to Singapore. I also have discovered the unknowns—the things I don't know, or won't know—but understanding the gaps have allowed me to have a good idea of the whole picture. Like missing a few pieces of a puzzle, it's annoying to not have the full image, but I can make out what should be there. It may not be detailed and exact, but it's there.

In 2016, one of my cousins, Gregory Kan, wrote a book of poetry called *This Paper Boat*. Through this book, I learned about my maternal grandfather, who I never had the chance to meet, as he passed away before I was born. We referred to him as Kong Kong. When I was a kid, my mother had a black-and-white picture of him on her dressing table. I remember the mornings I would wake up early and I could hear her drying her hair before she left early to catch the train into London. I can feel the warmth of the hairdryer and the smell of the hot filament, like the old electric heater my father used to pull out and use in emergencies. I sat on her bed watching her put on her make-up.

Every now and again, looking at the picture of Kong Kong. I would look at the picture intently, learning the contours of his face, drawing out the resemblance to my mother, and to me. He had smooth skin and pronounced cheekbones. His hair was jet black, with no hints of grey in the photo. It was a professionally taken photo—I'm not sure of the occasion, and he was alone, not with my grandma, who we called Ma Ma, nor with my mother or her siblings. It was always nice waking up early and hearing my mother still at home. When I was growing up, she didn't talk much about Kong Kong, just that he'd passed away while she was in her teens. It was only after reading Greg's book that the conversation opened.

Kong Kong had travelled to Singapore by boat from Guangzhou to find work in the 1930s. He left his wife behind, deciding to pave the way alone, so that she could follow him once he had found a job. Over time, they lost touch—at that time, no telephones to call each other, no Facebook or Google. From my mother's age and the age of her siblings, I guess the separation could be a consequence of the Japanese occupation of Singapore in the 1940s. I guess over time, he must have lost hope of ever seeing her again. He eventually met a Chinese lady in Singapore—my Ma Ma. They fell in love and had 10 children, my mother being number 7. Two were adopted into other families—something I understand was not uncommon in those days—and I am grateful that these sisters have since been reunited and are part of the family again. One day, I'm sure to Kong Kong's surprise, his first wife appeared in Singapore. She had been looking for him for many years. I guess she didn't expect to find him with a new wife and many children and I wonder what conversations were had when that happened: Kong Kong's realisation that he suddenly had two wives; his first wife's realisation that her husband had moved on and fathered many, many children; her elation and heartbreak at finally finding him; my Ma Ma, suddenly meeting her husband's first wife. Did she know he was previously married? Was she jealous? Did she feel compassion?

What I do know is that my grandparents were kind. It would have been too easy to say, "Sorry—I've moved on," and for Kong Kong's first wife to return back to China, heartbroken. Instead, they took her in, and supported her for the rest of her life. Kong Kong and Ma Ma went to live in the Chinese medicine shop that he owned and my Kong Kong's first wife moved into the family home, where my great-grandmother, who we called Lao-Ma, lived, too. Kong Kong's first wife took care of my mother and seven of her nine siblings. She became known to us grandchildren as "Spectacle Ma Ma", because, well, she wore dark rimmed spectacles. I remember her wearing a lot of brown or beige, and I don't have many memories of interacting with her. I'm not sure when she passed away, but her ashes rest alongside those of Lao Ma and Ma Ma at Mandai Columbarium.

I have never had the opportunity to go to China, to experience first-hand some of my maternal heritage line. I would love to visit Guangzhou, knowing that Kong Kong was from there, and have researched and read up on the region. It was probably about 80 or even 90 years ago when he left there and, judging by the city's rapid modernisation, it will be very different now, compared to when he lived there, but I like to think I will feel connected to some of the people and their culture.

Ma Ma came to stay with us in the UK one time. It was the only time I really spent with her. Her English wasn't so good, but I remember her smile and I remember studying her face, assessing which parts looked like my mother. I remember she was kind. I was still quite young, maybe 7 or 8 years old. One time visiting Singapore, I had to communicate with her through one of my cousins, who translated both ways. She passed away when I was 13 years old. My older sister flew to Singapore with my mum for the funeral. I remember being sad that I never got to know her very well. It was probably the first time I felt there was a part of my history I wanted to know better. My memories of her and those feelings of loss have returned a few times since living in Singapore and are accentuated by being away from my own mother. My kids miss her (and my father) and I have to consider that one of the decisions we made in moving back to Singapore was to put physical distance between us and our family.

In contrast to my mother's huge family, my father is an only child. My grandpa was an accountant and at age 33 gave up his successful post to become a Christian minister. He is a *Baba*—the term given to Peranakan males. He was born in Malacca, Malaysia, and was the third of four boys. His father, my Ah-Kong, used to wear a three-piece suit and a hat, too. He took my grandpa to watch cricket being played at the Padang, a big grassy field in the centre of Singapore, which is still home to a cricket club today. My grandma worked for the

Singapore government and was secretary for various different ambassadors and MPs, including the late President Nathan. On one of our family holidays to Singapore, I think in 2000, I thought my father must have been in trouble when my grandma received a phone call and then told him, "The President wants to see you." President Nathan remembered my father from when he was a youngster and wanted to say hello.

My grandma had a successful career with the Singaporean government, being posted in Canberra, Moscow and London. She has some amazing stories about serving in these places and she had a real adventure. As a Singaporean, the Russian winters in Moscow were the coldest weather she had ever experienced, but she says her top-floor apartment was well insulated. Once, she left her home feeling warm and comfortable. She locked her apartment door behind her and got into the elevator, taking her down to the ground floor. She opened the front door out onto the street and was suddenly hit with the biting cold, and realised she was only wearing one layer! Grandma had a government-provided car that carried her around. Once, she got a little lost and the next thing she knew, she was pulled over by a non-uniformed officer. She wound down the window and he pointed, saying, "that way, madam"—always being watched, always followed by the Soviet government.

Last year, Grandma gifted me her beautiful medal of long service to the nation. It sits upon black velvet in a red box. I feel honoured, if not a little inadequate to now possess it and I will treasure it with pride forever. My grandpa was one of four sons, while my grandma was adopted at a young age. She recently told me that she was adopted twice. First by a lady who became the mistress to the man who became her adopted father. He brought her into his family, where she had an older sister. My grandma speaks of her second adopted mother as a very kind lady who loved her like her own. It touches my heart to think of the love her adopted mother must have had and I like to think of the charm my grandma would have shown as a little girl to be accepted into the family. My grandma says she had no desire to find her birth parents, just that she was so grateful for the family she found herself in. She continues to live in this beautiful posture of gratitude at the age of 92, along with my grandpa in their home in Punggol, in the east of Singapore.

My mother is Teochew Chinese. There are certain Teochew foods I recognise, but I don't think much of the culture has been passed down to me or my sisters. When I was growing up, my paternal grandma was posted to London, and so we had greater influence from the Peranakan side of the family. I would like to know more about my Teochew heritage and even now as I write, I am thinking of a couple of Teochew restaurants I know in Singapore and when I can visit them. I am unaware of Teochew traditions, its history and the language. I mean, I know there is a dialect, but I can't speak it and I can't identify it.

I mentioned having to own the label of "Chinese" when I was at school in the UK. I really didn't like the label. It was something I couldn't own and something I felt forced to wear and I think that this was probably the main reason why the Teochew heritage took a back seat to the Peranakan. My Teochew heritage comes directly from China, whereas the

Peranakan heritage, while it has Chinese roots, is one that can be geographically and culturally pinpointed to the Straits area of Singapore and Malaysia.

During my childhood, certain Peranakan foods became treats to look forward to, usually during Chinese New Year, or when we visited Singapore for holidays. Laksa, kueh salat, kueh lapis and Nyonya rice dumplings were all favourites. As my sisters and I grew older, our understanding of our Peranakan heritage grew, learning about the mix of Chinese, locals and Europeans (mainly Portuguese and Dutch) in this melting pot of culture. But despite this, I still remained ignorant with regards to the Peranakan way, its customs and its traditions.

We made some Portuguese friends in the two years we were living in Surrey, in the south of England, before coming to live in Singapore. An amazing family, Paul, Ruth, and their three children, Kevin, Reuben and Sophia. The first time we met we bonded over barbequed food and my secret recipe for belly pork marinade. Over time we would go to each other's houses every other week on a Friday night and cook for each other our local delights. I cooked laksa, chicken rice, nasi lemak, rendang and Singapore curry. We shared steamboat and we cooked bak kut teh. Strangely, we would find that there were some similarities between Singaporean cuisine and Portuguese cuisine, including a very similar Portuguese dish to bak kut teh. We realised that the Portuguese had shared and borrowed some customs and dishes in the days when they inhabited Malacca in the 1500s and 1600s.

I started to become more aware of the Peranakan culture in my Singaporean surroundings, also researching a little here and there on the internet. The Peranakans have a rich culture and blended heritage. Its food culture is widespread in modern Singapore and as I became more aware of the traditions and styles, Peranakan shop houses and batik prints suddenly seemed like they were everywhere. I don't know if you've experienced this before, but when you buy a new car, suddenly, you see the same model everywhere! It was like that for me, but with Peranakan patterns, colours, food and buildings. I even stumbled across Peranakan culture on TV! One evening, Millie and I were sitting down to find something on Netflix, and we spotted the series, *The Little Nyonya,* a television series filmed in 2008, but set between the 1930s and 2000s. We watched it, learning a bit about the old Peranakan lifestyle and took in the decor, outfits and even the mindsets and struggles of the Peranakans of the time.

Scouring the internet for more information on my Peranakan heritage became a bit of a habit and one day, I came across an article written by a local Singaporean author, Josephine Chia. Her article outlined her feelings about being Peranakan, not Chinese. This resonated with me, having experienced the same thoughts and feelings while I was growing up in the UK, with friends being very familiar with China and the Chinese, but no idea what Peranakan heritage was. I reached out to her and to my surprise, heard back from her, offering to meet to talk more about my interest in my Peranakan heritage. Over the following few days I researched and found out that she had lived in the UK for many years, staying close to where I had grown up in Surrey. I was excited to hear what she might have been able to share, having written a couple of books about her old *kampong*, even winning the Singapore Literary Prize in 2014 with her book, *Kampong Spirit*.

We met at a cafe in a central shopping mall. Having never met her and having to wear face masks due to the ongoing COVID-19 pandemic regulations, I approached the cafe looking at everyone who passed, trying to make eye contact and somehow communicate that I was here to meet someone. I spotted a lady in full Peranakan clothing, a light blue ornate *sarong kebaya* and even *kasut manik*, the traditional beaded shoes of Peranakan women. Her hair was a smooth white, cut into a neat bob. I walked towards her and said hello. Her accent was immediately Singaporean, and for some reason this took me by surprise. Having spent so long in the UK, I had imagined her voice to sound perhaps like my mum's—Singaporean phrases with British embellishments. Josephine held herself confidently yet gracefully as she walked toward a table and we sat down.

It was dinner time, around 6.30pm, but I had managed to pop home between finishing work and meeting Josephine and so I had grabbed something quick to eat. The cafe served some light bites and when Josephine said she hadn't yet eaten, I was keen for her to have something. On the menu was "chicken curry Cornish pasty". The traditional Singapore curry puff is said to have its origins in the British Cornish pasty and we found it funny that this cafe's menu seemed to have gone full circle. Josephine insisted I share the pasty with her, with a tone that reminded me of my grandma: it was an offer, but with no option to say no! I agreed and we ordered.

The food and some coffees arrived, allowing us to take our masks off. Josephine's face showed her to be younger than her grey hair initially suggested and her youthfulness was evident in the way she spoke and held herself. I later found out that she runs workshops with young people, inspiring them to write. I could see how she could engage a younger generation with her liveliness and passion. Josephine showed interest in my journey of self-discovery, asking me questions and listening intently. She shared photos and gave me insights into my Peranakan heritage. She told me about how she grew up in a *kampong* in Potong Pasir, an area I know fairly well—I work right next to the MRT station. Potong Pasir has, of course, changed a lot since Josephine lived there. She told me about her parents and about her desire to go to school. Her father had been displeased with the idea of her gaining an education, but her mother was more supportive. So Josephine would accompany her mother, selling nasi lemak around the neighbourhood to earn enough money for her to be able to go to school.

Josephine was incredibly passionate about her Peranakan identity—not just in Singapore, but when she was living in the UK, too, attending events in her *sarong kebaya*, even in the harsh cold of the British winter. She passed me magazines and leaflets and encouraged me to join The Peranakan Association of Singapore. I loved speaking with her and listening to her stories. Josephine told me about how she began to write and that she gained inspiration from living in the UK, in the neighbourhood of some literary legends. And there I was with a literary legend in her own right, listening to her describe her passions—so much of which she had included in her writings. She inspired me. I went home and started to write a book—this book.

***

In the build-up to the Lunar New Year of 2021, Millie and I had decided we would try to get traditional Peranakan clothing for us to wear to our various gatherings over the opening weekend. I had learned from Josephine that Peranakan heritage is passed down through the father's line, and when I mentioned this to Millie, she was excited to take on the identity of a Nyonya (a Peranakan woman). She looked graceful and most elegant in her first *sarong kebaya*. I watched with a sense of pride as the aunties at the shop fussed over her, measuring her up and helping her to choose which *kebaya* to buy. Aspen had a turn to choose too, and the aunties again fussed over her, and even measured her up for a face mask to match her sarong. She looked as elegant as her mother, and did her best to hold herself with equal grace. If you know Aspen, you'll understand this was hard, as she is incredibly active and loves a bit of rough and tumble too, but she clearly sensed the occasion and how special it was to wear the traditional clothing of her heritage. Milo and I chose our batik shirts and we looked the part. I felt a sense of pride: elements of my heritage uncovered and learned, and my whole family embracing the Peranakan culture. Each occasion on which we wore our sarong kebayas and batik shirts we would receive looks and kind comments about how lovely it was to see, particularly Millie and Aspen, in traditional clothing. I hope my kids will remember these moments as they grow up and hopefully maintain that connection to their heritage.

Through the process of learning about and embracing our newly found heritage, Millie found a private collection-cum-museum and managed to book us into a visit at The Intan museum—the home of Alvin Yapp, a *Baba* (Peranakan man), in the Joo Chiat area. It was a sunny day, one of those days where the humidity is lower, giving a more Mediterranean feel to the side streets. We arrived and took our shoes off outside, walking into the darker indoors. Back when this row of houses were built, there was tax on windows and so fewer windows were fitted to keep costs down. This seemed to help the temperature and indoors felt cool. There were also increased taxes on wider properties and so many of the houses of the era (including this one) were long and narrow terraces. I have heard stories of Peranakan children learning to ride their bicycles indoors, going from the front to the back of their homes as it was long and straight. The front of the house was decorated with many pot plants, hanging baskets and a wooden ladder, the latter seemingly with no purpose. In the UK, we'd have been concerned that we had left it for the easy use of a burglar to get into the house!

On entering the terraced house, we were overwhelmed by Alvin's vast collection of Peranakan decor. Some of the beautiful and well-kept vintage collection gave me a fresh understanding as I hadn't known that these items were specifically Peranakan. Spittoons and *tingkats* lined the stairs, ornate furniture was spread over the whole open-planned downstairs. Plates, bowls, spoons and dishes were lined up along shelves. The floor tiles were original, but they reminded me of the floor tiles in my old pastor's house. I had helped to clean them after they had been laid. I remember the way the golden brown colours would start to shine through as we scrubbed the dirt away. We walked beyond the entrance way and looked around the home, eyes wide, darting from side to side and up and down, struggling to take in everything around us. There were tapestries hanging on walls, plates, dishes, artwork and more on every surface, even hanging from the ceiling. To the right was an upright piano, upon which rested many award trophies, showing off The Intan's many accolades. In the entrance area were two wooden armchairs—more like thrones, really. These were interlaced with mother of pearl and were simply stunning pieces of furniture. I was surprised anyone ever sat on them! Between the two armchairs was what looked like a car number plate, which read "THE INTAN" in bold, capital letters. It was the only thing that seemed out of place in the otherwise perfectly laid out house-museum.

Alvin stood, proudly in front of a big wooden dresser near the arm chairs, and passionately explained the desire—no, the *obsession* that Peranakans had with maintaining authentic culture. I could see this trait in Alvin, as he spoke about his collection and educated us on the way of the Peranakans. The Peranakans of old were desperate to hold on to their Chinese origins, but also desperate to show how they belonged in their westernised world. I guess there are some of these traits in me—less of an obsession, but still, a curiosity to discover and a desire to know and uphold. Perhaps I am a more authentic Peranakan than I originally thought.

There were a few other people gathering as part of the tour of Alvin's home, and we were invited to sit around a large coffee table in his living area, which was dressed with ornate vases, each unique, with hand painted designs. His passion was evident and as he shared with us his love for all things Peranakan. He started collecting Peranakan items from the age of 17 years old. Alvin's eccentricity did not impact on his approachability— he was friendly, kind and warm. We were in his home—his bedroom was upstairs in a section that was not open to the public—but he was so welcoming and took time to carefully answer every question posed to him. While he spoke, I couldn't help but look all around, taking in the sights and trying to glean whatever I could about my ancestors and my heritage. Alvin took us upstairs to his vast collection of beaded shoes, as well as more furniture and fabrics. The wall along the staircase had some beautiful tapestries on them—embroidered fabrics, every picture or pattern created with little stitches, every stitch entered by hand, just like the beads on the shoes. Alvin shared that he had currently over 270 pairs of shoes, some he had only brought into his collection recently, as his collection continues to grow. Some of these shoes were in such great condition, that they looked brand new!

Downstairs, the long thin house had a kitchen and toilet at the back. In Norwich, where Millie and I met and were married, there are typical 18th and 19th century terraced houses, which have their bathrooms downstairs at the back of the house. I remember needing the toilet in the middle of the night and lying in bed for a good 10 minutes, deciding whether I really wanted to navigate in the dark down the steep stairs, through the dining room into the kitchen to finally get to the toilet. I hoped Alvin wasn't as clumsy as I am when I am tired and dopey, because the *tingkats* and spittoons on the stairs were an obstacle in the light of day, let alone at night! The bathroom was decorated with beautiful ornate tiles—a key feature of Peranakan heritage. These were once all hand-painted with Chinese style flowers and birds, and provided decoration to a Peranakan home. Nowadays, Peranakan tiles are very popular and are made en-masse, with the pictures being printed by machine.

Our kids paid a lot of interest in our visit to The Intan. Their understanding of their Peranakan heritage is quite new and I think it intrigues them. I guess the thing that will develop over time is their understanding of it being *their* heritage, and their personalisation of it. Before we left, Alvin treated Aspen to a performance of the traditional Malay song, *Burung Kakak Tua*, or "Older Sister Bird", which he played on his piano. He played with passion, feeling and skill. Entertaining in the moment, but also reminiscent of the past. Aspen watched, entranced by the music which rang through the house.

***

I have mixed feelings about our visit to The Intan that day. Don't get me wrong—I loved it. Alvin was amazing and the collection is genuinely priceless. But there was something strange about seeing my culture and heritage in a museum. I am a Peranakan now. I understand there are fears that the Peranakan people and heritage are dying out—Peranakans are marrying people from other cultural backgrounds and so traditions are being lost through the generations. And that's fine. After all, the Peranakans all came about from the Chinese marrying locals and the locals were mixed with Europeans after their occupation of Malacca— by definition, the Peranakan way was a modernisation of even older traditions. Some are quite happy for the Peranakans to fade into the history books, whereas others are trying to promote and rekindle the Peranakan lifestyle and maintain the heritage. One of the ways of doing this was by opening The Intan as a museum. But that is what I find strange. Can you really keep heritage alive by placing it in a museum? I believe it is so important to have museums, to remind us of where we have come from, but I think museums keep things in the past.

I love my Peranakan heritage and I would love to see it flourishing—particularly the food. I can see that in modern Singapore, it is hard to maintain some of the customs and traditions and so perhaps we need to redefine what a Peranakan is—not to change, or recreate, but just to redefine, perhaps to emphasise different aspects and from these strengths, develop the modern Peranakan. These could be in the clothing styles— *batik* shirts for the men and pretty lace adornments for the ladies are so easy to make more current and modern. It could come in the pride that Peranakans take in knowing their heritage and passing on this understanding to their children. I'm sure these are things that people are already doing, but a fresh emphasis could help to see the Peranakan heritage remain, rather than become absorbed into more clearly defined cultures of today.

I understand that some Peranakan clothing is being incorporated into more modern clothing styles and outfits recently, with more people wearing traditional items of clothing with modern twists. Some women wear *kebayas* with jeans and men feel comfortable to wear their *batik* shirts with shorts. Some of these people have come under scrutiny by the older generations, who felt this modernisation was damaging the traditional way. But if Peranakan traditions don't move with the times, perhaps all that will be left of the Peranakan heritage will be in museums and historians will be the only ones who know about the culture and traditions. Perhaps a balance between the traditional and the modern is what is needed.

I am beginning to understand that heritage can also be a personal thing. For me, I don't know everything there is to know about my Peranakan or Teochew heritage, not even close—but I feel a deep and personal connection to it. Due to my British upbringing, I have fusion versions of each culture: British-Peranakan and British-Teochew. Living in Singapore has given the Teochew and Peranakan aspects a greater emphasis, and this continues to grow the more I learn; but perhaps authentic culture is the one to which you are most true and for me, this means a collection of different influences.

After all, the Peranakan culture was born from its own fusion of traditions and cultures. This fusion, I believe, does not disqualify the authenticity of a person's belonging. It can be diluted or mixed or fused. I have realised through this journey of self-discovery that I can be Peranakan *and* Teochew *and*

European. I *am* Singaporean *and* I am British. This blending does not dilute authenticity, but the differing and sometimes contrasting aspects and traditions add variety and flavour to my life. While sometimes I feel like I do not belong to any of my cultures, it is important for me to embrace my Peranakan-Teochew-Singaporean-Britishness by learning about each aspect and living authentically, understanding that I can call all of these cultures mine.

Chapter 7

Suppressing the Inner Asian Parent

It was a warm, hazy, but comfortable evening at the Supertree Grove at the Gardens by the Bay. Harvest Moon festival was in full flow, with lanterns giving off a soft glow as the sun set over Singapore. The Supertrees were lit a deep red colour and atmospheric music was playing through the outdoor speakers, giving off a calm vibe. There was hardly anyone around when we arrived. This being our first Harvest Moon festival in Singapore, we assumed this was either normal, or that the COVID-19 regulations had caused people to stay at home and celebrate on their own. Lantern installations had been put up around various parts of the gardens and we and the children were excited to tick off all of the boxes on an activity sheet they were given, and experience all of the displays. Throughout the evening we were made very aware of the regulations—signs told us to maintain a safe distance from each other and audio announcements regularly rolled round, reminding visitors to wear masks at all times, even when taking photos. I intentionally use the word "regulations", rather than "restrictions", as I honestly believe that the laws and advice are to help society function as best as possible. I may not agree with every decision made by governments and I may sometimes feel restricted, but it's a fair price to pay for reduced deaths and some sort of freedom.

That night, at the Supertree Grove, Aspen, aged 5, found the regulations just too restrictive. She wanted to take her mask off so she could smile properly for a photo. That was all. And I understood her frustration. But the signs were clear, specifically stating that the rule included photo-taking and there were staff walking around to ensure people adhered to the rules. The crowds had started to arrive too, as darkness had fallen and the lanterns were in full glow. We, of course, wanted to honour the ruling and keep people safe, but there was an added pressure after hearing in the news about several expats deliberately disobeying the laws and receiving hefty fines and having their work visas revoked.

I remember feeling like a thousand eyes were looking at us. The reality is that probably only 20 people were within earshot and most of those probably knew what it was like to have a kid disagree about something! After all, Aspen wasn't just choosing to be defiant for the sake of it—she loved the displays and she was so happy to see the lanterns glowing that she wanted a photo with her mask off. We tried our hardest to explain to Aspen that it wasn't safe, that there were rules and guidelines, and that there were clear consequences for us disobeying the rules, but it just made things worse. She began to get cross and shout. We remained calm, trying to explain, to distract or to pacify, but all the while, Aspen's frustration was escalating. Eventually she decided she wanted to run away from us, and with the crowds thickening, we feared for her safety. We were in a standoff. She wanted to stay and have her photo taken with no mask, and we weren't allowing her to.

Millie was beginning to feel frustrated and Milo was keen to explore more of the lanterns, so they went ahead; but this aggravated Aspen even more and she started to back off towards the lanterns she wanted the photo with—but to get there she was walking backwards into the crowds. Like catching wild rabbits in my university days (very unsuccessfully, especially after a few beers!), I edged close enough to think I could get a hold of her before she ran off. I got her hand! Immediately, she started to try to pull away, so I held her a little tighter, and asked her to stay close and stay safe and that we were going to find Mummy. After a bit of wrestling, Aspen calmed down, and we walked together to catch up with Millie and Milo. The rest of the evening was lovely. Situation diffused, more lanterns to be seen and two happy kids. For any parents reading this, I guess you can relate, and you probably have some very similar accounts.

On the busy but quiet MRT on the way home, Millie saw what looked like purple pen marks on Aspen's hand. On closer inspection, it wasn't ink at all. In my desperation to keep hold of her, I had marked my daughter's skin. I was devastated. I was embarrassed. I felt guilty. Fortunately for her it was just surface marks, no deep bruising—the colour was more likely caused by friction from sweaty hands and from my gripping too hard. Nonetheless, my eyes welled up as I apologised to her when putting her to bed that night. I couldn't believe I had done that to her and played the scenario over and over again in my head, trying to find a different way I could have helped her, or addressed the situation, without squeezing her hand so tight. Over the following few weeks I found myself disengaging with discipline—I allowed both of our kids to get away with more as I felt guilty for what I had done, and fearful that I would do it again.

Looking back on that night at Gardens by the Bay, I can confidently say that my actions were OK—I did what I could to keep Aspen safe. I even spoke to one of the school counsellors about it. But what I noticed, and I continue to notice, is that over the years as a parent, I have felt super aware of feelings that may provoke unreasonable discipline. It bubbles beneath the surface and boils when I get frustrated about particular things. I feel like I have to control my inner-Asian parent.

***

I am pretty sure I had a happy childhood. I say it with a level of certainty, and perhaps a level of uncertainty, because I can clearly remember events and things we got up to, but I can't immediately connect to these things emotionally. My parents and I have a fantastic relationship, I would say they are among my closest friends, who offer wise advice and unconditional love. They try to understand when my thoughts or experiences come from an unexpected direction. They continue to embrace my friends as part of the family, just as they did when I was growing up. They are interesting and fun. But when I look at my own children and the children who I encounter everyday as a teacher, I don't know whether I was a kid who really *enjoyed* life. Perhaps I was, but there was a tangible feeling of displacement at times, but I thought everyone felt it. I certainly didn't really appreciate my childhood until I was in my early or even mid-20s, and looking back, I was so fortunate. I just don't remember feeling it at the time.

For some reason, I remember my fourth birthday vividly. We took the train from Stoneleigh train station into London and spent the day at London Zoo. I don't remember the zoo from that day, but I remember the train. You could approach the train station two different ways. Stoneleigh Broadway was a wide street with shops either side, leading towards the train station. On the other side of the train tracks was what seemed like the end of the road, with more shops and a couple of restaurants. We would usually approach the station from the Broadway side, but on my birthday, we parked on the other side. It was rainy and dark when our train pulled into the station. The road glowed with the orange street lights. We walked out of the station and turned to our right, where there was a Chinese restaurant. We went in for my birthday meal and had frog's legs, among other things. It must have been a really fun day for me to remember it so well. That evening, I have another memory that is clear in my mind.

I was late in giving up my dummy, or pacifier. I'm not sure why and I'm sure I must have expressed some defiance in getting rid of it. The evening of my fourth birthday, I stood in the kitchen, next to the bin that I remember being about chest height. The bin was half full and it was time for me to throw my dummy away. My mother tells me she kept a couple spare for a few weeks in case I regressed, but she never needed to use them.

Ages four to six is pretty blank, with no memories from that time until Lita, our helper, moved away. And then there was a period from about six years old where I experienced extreme unreasonable parenting, not from my parents, but from my grandpa.

Grandpa and Grandma were living in the UK, and Grandma had recently retired from working for the government. They helped my parents out by taking us to and from school and cooking dinner, too. Grandma's dinners were, and remain, legendary. She was an amazing cook, and would always cook just too much—we could finish it all, but it was enough for everyone to feel slightly uncomfortable at the end of the meal! One evening we were sitting at the table, eating dinner. Most of the family were finished and it was coming to the end of the meal. I took some food from the dish in the middle of the table and instead of first putting it on my plate, I put it straight into my mouth. The evening went on, and I assumed nothing was wrong, but the next morning, my grandpa turned up to take us to school and he was in a rage. He told me how disrespectful it was and he made me feel horribly guilty, with no space for redemption. This wasn't an isolated incident. This feeling of guilt and fear I had of him came quite regularly—a messy bedroom, a wrong action, a wrong choice of words. Every time I felt worse.

It may seem contradictory for a Christian minister to behave this way, but I guess some denominations focus on the rules, regulations and discipline, rather than the unconditional love and grace, that I think actually defines Christianity. Grandpa has had quite an eventful life and as an adult, I can understand some of the reasons behind his intensity and strictness.

Born in 1928, it was just before his 14th birthday when the Japanese occupied Singapore with ruthless force. Still today, at 93 years old, Grandpa can recollect some of his experiences under the Japanese. One time, all of the men in Grandpa's village (now Tiong Bahru) were lined up and some Japanese soldiers separated them into two groups. The soldiers used swords to direct the men into two different lines. Grandpa was moved to the left, separated from his dad and his three brothers, Harry, Charlie and Albert, who were moved to the right. They didn't understand what the soldiers were asking of them, they simply obeyed the physical directions. All of a sudden, one soldier stopped and pointed at Grandpa with his sword. He signalled for Grandpa to join the other line with his brothers. Immediately after this, the men in the other line were taken away at gunpoint to be killed at Changi beach, an incident known as the Changi Beach Massacre. I can't imagine the trauma that would have caused and back in the 1940s there wasn't any awareness of mental health, nor the science or systems to be able to help.

I know none of this can excuse this behaviour toward an eight-year-old boy, but knowing some of what my Grandpa had to live through has helped me to understand him a little more and has really helped in my journey of forgiving him and loving him.

Grandpa is Peranakan. The origins of the Peranakans date back as far as the 15th century, when Chinese people began to settle in Malaysia (then called Malaya). The Peranakans had their golden age during the late 1800s and early 1900s, where they were a prominent group in the region, holding influential jobs and status. Over time, the locals had intermarried with western settlers too, mainly from Portugal and the Netherlands. The Peranakan culture developed out of this melting pot of influences and has a very wide and blended heritage. I understand that during the golden age, Peranakan men in particular felt a huge pressure to uphold Chinese values, while also balancing this with their western culture. I find this particularly interesting as I had my own version of this, growing up in the UK. Perhaps, despite my physical distance from the region and from the traditions of the *Babas* (the name given to Peranakan men), I have been living a fairly authentic Peranakan life.

Grandpa's strict discipline was displayed on a regular basis and I remember being smacked, yelled at and I remember an aching feeling I had in the pit of my gut. One day, I cried so much that my torso, from my throat down to my stomach, hurt. I would dread the mornings with Grandpa when he arrived to take us to school, my only motivation being that once we arrived at school, I was away from him for the rest of the day until pick-up. I even remember feeling a physical dread towards the end of my school day. I am aware that much of this may have contributed to my behavioural issues at school and the subsequent decision that I wouldn't complete my education at that particular school.

It all came to a head one day. As normal, my Pa would leave for work and as normal, and Grandpa would find something he could be upset about. This particular morning it was about the tidiness of my room—or should I say, the lack of tidiness of my room. He became very aggravated, yelling at me, belittling me.

This continued as we got into his car and as we drove down the road. We hadn't long ago moved house and so my parents had transferred my sister, Amanda, to a different primary school to me. We went to drop her off first. As Grandpa turned into the school car park, he took the corner a bit too tightly and scraped the side of his white Honda Concerto on the sky-blue painted gate. Grandpa really looked after his car. He stored a car-cleaning kit in the back of the car and would keep it buffed and clean.

The scrape made a really nasty sound. I can still see him turning round from the front of the car to look at me in the back. "This is your fault!" he shouted at me. "If only you would just tidy your room!" I remember beginning to well up, but trying my hardest to fight the tears back. "No wonder I love your sisters but I don't love you!" These words pierced my heart. I cried an uncontrollable cry.

After my younger sister, Amanda, got out, the next stop was my older sister's school. As Charmaine got out of the car, I remember the way she looked at me with a face of helplessness, like she was saying sorry, but couldn't do anything to make me feel better. I looked back through tearful eyes and she closed the door. I don't remember Grandma trying to comfort me on the 10 minute drive to my school. She largely remained silent when Grandpa told me off. His words kept coming throughout the journey, between the silence and my sniffs that, to me, echoed in the car.

I hadn't managed to stop my tears when I got to school and the comfort of a few friends on the playground forced out a few large outbursts—pain and heartache leaking out. I wasn't able to tell them what had happened as I was ashamed, perhaps of Grandpa, perhaps of myself, but more likely a combination of the two. I remember my teacher Mrs Thompson asking me what the matter was. Through tears and hyperventilation, I lied and told her my cat had died. We had a cat, Tigger, and come to think of it, I don't remember when she died or how, but this seemed like a plausible reason, and one I wouldn't have to explain. Mrs Thompson wasn't particularly comforting and asked me if I'd rather go home. I knew that wasn't a choice as my only home option was to go home with Grandpa and spend the day with him. The rest of the school day was a bit of a blur, but I remember hearing my friends explaining my tears to other peers, "His cat died this morning", and the cover-up explanation being received fairly well. It was later that academic year that I left that school, my misbehaviour no longer tolerated.

I can't recollect how I got home that afternoon—I imagine my grandparents came to pick me up as normal. I do remember dinner that night. It was just my parents and us kids and my father asked how our day was. I burst into tears, explaining what had happened in the morning. He was shocked at my response and looked at Charmaine for confirmation that my account was accurate. She nodded. My father was angry. He muttered some words, along the lines of "I've had enough of this", and left the dining room. I'm not sure what time of year it was, but I remember him putting his coat on. It must have been around 7pm.

I'm not sure what was the effect of the fall-out of this situation. But over the years I have learned to forgive and I have learned to love my Grandpa again. I remember not seeing my grandparents for a little while (they moved back to Singapore for a few years), and there was one day we went to collect them from the airport. When I saw them, I was suddenly taller than them. I must have been 12 or 13, as I vividly remember wearing my England football shirt—the yellow goalkeeper one that David Seaman wore for Euro 1996. David Seaman was the hero of England's 1996 campaign, saving the crucial penalty in the post-extra time decisive shootout against Spain, who were big favourites. I even remember the headlines the next morning in the national paper, SEAMAN SINKS SPANISH ARMADA! A few years later, my grandparents moved back to Singapore and I didn't see them much afterwards. Perhaps it gave me time to heal.

Looking back with my knowledge and understanding as a trained educator, I realise that what I suffered from Grandpa would now be classified as emotional abuse and I am surprised that my teacher, Mrs Thompson, didn't spot any signs that there was something else going on, rather than misbehaviour. I'm glad that educators are better trained and more aware these days. It was painful and there are some consequences from those times that will probably be with me for life. My low self-esteem stayed with me for a long time, and truthfully, still sits in the background of my life these days. But I am grateful for being aware and knowing how to cope with it now.

Today, my grandparents live in a small HDB apartment in Punggol, in the northeast of Singapore. I visit them regularly and love spending time with them. Grandpa loves to play chess with my son, his great-grandson, Milo, and he is grateful for every opportunity we have to share time together. I wonder whether he remembers those times and whether he thought he was in the wrong. I wonder if he wrestled with it, whether he regretted the way he acted out, seemingly uncontrollably. Grandma actually tried to bring it up recently, saying, "Grandpa used to be very strict with you, do you remember?"

I replied with "Of course, how would I forget? But it's all in the past now—that was a long time ago." I think she was hoping to bring reconciliation to any unsettled feelings, or perhaps to help Grandpa to see his faults in his old age and I appreciated it, but it was unnecessary. It really was a long time ago and I have forgiven Grandpa—a process that wasn't easy, but has allowed us to have a wonderful, loving relationship today.

***

Asian parents seem to have an international reputation. In the UK, Asian parents were the strictest parents, whose focus was their child's education beyond their wellbeing. Asian parents were the ones who disciplined their children with a cane, slipper or belt and the ones who yelled the most. Asian kids were the ones who were most studious and who would be disappointed by achieving 95 per cent in an exam, wondering where they went wrong in the 5 per cent. The Asian kids didn't do playdates—weekends were for extra studying. Over the years, I have met many Asians—Indians, Chinese, Japanese, Koreans and more—who can all relate to the difficulties of receiving "Asian parenting", and there's a knowing look we share when one is reminded of an occasion.

My parents were a combination of Asian and Christian. I can see now that their "Asian" parenting style was fairly mild compared to many, if not all, of my friends and family here in Singapore. But growing up in the UK, their strictness and discipline was magnified by our context. My grandpa's discipline was actually fairly in-keeping with some of what I have heard here in Singapore, with many of my friends in their 20s, 30s and 40s, feeling like the parenting they received was unreasonable and too heavy-handed. A Malaysian friend of mine is actually living with her fiancée and her father doesn't even know she has a boyfriend, as she is concerned about him disapproving and subsequently, what he might say or do. Before my teens I would say my parents were fairly strict, but also very loving. My sisters and I all played musical instruments growing up, and I remember being forced to practice my 'cello and the pressure from my eight-hours-of-practice-a-day music college graduate of a father! (As a parent now, knowing how much these lessons cost, I can sympathise a little more!).

I remember getting a hot bottom fairly regularly for misbehaving, but it wasn't all discipline. The best birthday party of my childhood wasn't one of my friends', nor was it an all-expenses covered sort of celebration either. It was my seventh birthday party and it was held in our garage. We actually kept our cars in the garage and the fact that we kept cars in the garage instead of "stuff" is actually very un-British. We played some simple but fun and engaging games that my father organised: dropping matchsticks into milk bottles and bursting balloons that were tied to our laces were my favourites that day. In the way that kids compare, I remember thinking to myself that day that no one had as cool a dad as I did.

British parents seemed a bit more relaxed and a bit lighter on discipline than mine. At least, much lighter on physical discipline. I didn't really hang out with tearaway kids, but they definitely had more trust and freedom than my parents allowed. Honestly, it's hard to identify clear differences, but it was something I felt regularly. An example that seems small now, but was huge to me at the time, was when my friends in Year 3 (2nd grade) were obsessed with English Premier League football sticker books. They would come to school with stacks of stickers that they'd swap and a magazine they would stick them into, trying to collect them all. I remember begging my parents to buy me some stickers, but to them, it was a waste of money. Eventually, my mum bought me a packet. I was so excited to open the pack, tearing it open to find, disappointingly, a measly five stickers inside. I must have been quite persuasive among my friends as I managed to swap ones for twos with some friends at school and eventually, I had a little stack of stickers myself. My parents wouldn't buy me the magazine. I can still picture it now, the 1993–1994 Premier League sticker book. It was blue with gold writing and had a picture of my favourite player on the front—Ryan Giggs. I think he actually might have been my favourite player *because* he was on the front of the book, as I didn't watch football, nor did I know much about it. But for me, it was a connection to my British friends and British culture that I hadn't had before.

One morning, I took the opportunity to acquire a sticker

book of my own. I was in the school playground—a typical British school playground—tarmac with hopscotch boxes and targets painted on the floor in white. It must have been raining the night before, as I can still picture the damp tarmac. There was a kid in my class, Gary. There were two Garys actually. One was a bit shorter with dark hair, and the other was skinny and blond. The skinny blond Gary was kind and I had no problem with him at all. In fact, I quite liked him. But as is the mind of a child, I somehow justified taking his nearly-complete sticker book and claiming it as my own. It was sitting on top of his bag in the playground as he kicked around a tennis ball with some other friends. I helped myself to it and played innocent when he noticed it had gone. When asked, I claimed it was my own, and poor Gary didn't confront me or accuse me.

The next day I brought the sticker book to school again, proudly showing off my collection, including many coveted *shinies*—the most sought after of all the stickers. Suddenly, I saw Gary's mother coming towards me at a pace. I remember feeling quite scared that I was going to be in lots of trouble. I'm not sure what she said, but she took the sticker book from me, handed it back to Gary and that was the end of that! I don't know what my parents thought as I'm pretty sure I showed it to them the night I brought it home and then the following day it was gone.

***

I completely understand (and fully believe) that the parenting I received was loving and I am truly grateful for my childhood.

Despite the Asian-style parenting of my own parents being quite mild, the combination of the contrast of western and eastern styles and my grandparents' involvement meant that some of my own learned parenting behaviours and defaults are not quite the way I would like them to be. I have found I need to be very conscious of my behaviours, which is, I guess, a good thing. Self-awareness is important to self-improvement and we strive to be the best parents we can for our kids.

My parents applied physical discipline by smacking us as kids (I don't think my older sister ever needed it, but I made up for that!), and my father had a stare that could sink warships. Their Christian faith and values were upheld with Asian-style and authority. We didn't really listen to secular pop music in the house—classical and jazz, yes, and also "Christian Pop" which, actually, isn't as bad as it sounds. Sometimes my friends will hear a song on the radio—Pink Floyd or the Rolling Stones or something well-known—and I'll have no idea what it is. They always remark: "But you're a musician! How do you not know that song!" My parents cared deeply about our influences and so we were even stopped from watching certain TV shows that may not have been in line with their values.

When I became a teenager, my headstrong stubbornness manifested itself as rebellion. I went out drinking and partying from the young age of 16 and my independence and freedom was not *given to* me, but *taken by* me. My parents and I argued a lot in my mid-teens and I rebelled against the Christian faith and my parents' values. As a parent now, I realise how difficult this would have been for them and while I was aware of my behaviours at the time, my striving for independence as a teenager was one that is common in that stage of youth.

***

I love being a dad. The day Milo was born, I wept with pride and excitement for this new stage in our life. We brought him home the day British tennis player, Andy Murray, won the Wimbledon men's singles title—one that hadn't been won by a Brit in 77 years. It was a hot summer, and I took advantage of this through skin-to-skin bonding with my son. Some days he'd fall asleep on my bare chest, while I'd stare at him for what felt like hours at a time. I decided to splash out on some bamboo linen muslins for him—the softest things I have ever felt, other than his cheeks. I hand-washed them and stood in the garden waving them in the warm sunlight to dry so he wouldn't be without one. He wasn't even two years old when Aspen was born. I felt that same wonder with her, watching her for hours on end—her tiny fingernails, her little mouth. Aspen slept for the first six months of her life. She was tired, growing, and loved to snooze whenever she could. I would sing to both of them every night—I still do—but back when they were just months old, I would hold them, head resting on my palms and their arms flopping either side of my forearm. They both would drift off peacefully before I laid them in their Moses basket that had been passed to us from my older sister after her daughter, Faith, had grown out of it.

These days, Millie and I take turns to have one-to-one time with each of our kids before they sleep and I remind them every day that I love them, that I am proud of them and that I am grateful to be their dad. Sometimes, I feel like parenthood comes naturally to me. I encourage my kids to try new things, and help them to feel confident when they are unsure. At other times I feel completely out of my depth. These moments come when they are rude, or when they are upset about… well, sometimes, nothing! Kids are like that. They can be super complicated—demanding something impossible at one moment, then taking pleasure in an old cardboard box in the next. These inconsistencies make parenting the hardest thing I have ever done—and continue to do!

I have learned that there are certain characteristics of Asian parenting that seem to be known the world over. First-hand, I have experienced a certain degree of strictness and unreasonableness—the latter being from grand-parenting. I have also had many conversations about this with local friends in Singapore, who have described experiences with their parents. Interestingly, very few parents I have spoken with are open to talking about their own parenting. Those who have opened up have explained a dislike for how hard they are on their children. Some parents have described themselves as "monsters" when it comes to their kids, but strangely, they seem to accept that it is just the way to be. Physical discipline is becoming less and less common in the UK and some see it as abuse. Recently, one of my neighbours, who is also a mother and from the UK, was in the elevator with a Singaporean parent, who was caning her son, forming red marks on his arm. He was only around four years old. She couldn't bear to allow this to happen and so took the cane from the mother, scolding her. Both mothers felt their action was justified and loving. This is an example of the stark contrast in western and Asian parenting, I suppose.

To my surprise, many of our Singaporean friends who do not yet have kids say that our parenting style is refreshing. They talk about the way we explain things to our kids, instead of just yelling at them; how we talk to them in calm tones; how we give consequences, not punishments. This offers great encouragement to me as these are traits we have intentionally built into our parenting. Some others may very well see us as "soft" and think our children lack discipline. There is also a difference between our private and public parenting, and so only a few closer friends will see us speak very firmly with our children. We want our children to behave well out of a desire to do the right thing, not out of a fear of embarrassment.

Sometimes I feel like I have to suppress the yelling, punishment and even the desire to smack our children when they are being particularly defiant or rude. We have decided not to smack our kids, by the way. (Telling a kid it's not good to hit another kid by hitting them just doesn't make sense.) I don't feel that being smacked as a child had a particularly bad or lasting effect on me, but it's not for us or our family. When we are out and they are not behaving in a particularly polite fashion, or if they forget their manners, I can really struggle with that, too. Some of this is my own pride—my insecurities about whether I am a good enough parent are exposed when the kids play up in public. I become very irritated when they don't appear to show appreciation or gratitude, particularly to Millie. Asians place a lot of emphasis on maintaining 'face', and I wonder whether the strong feelings I have about our children's lack of gratitude is to do with that.

I am continually learning that parenting is not prescriptive. Parenting books and manuals contradict other parenting books and manuals, which tells me that the ins and outs are not necessarily as important as consistent love and guidance—shining a torch in the dark turns of life, showing your kids the right way to go. We teach them values, and we create a particular family culture and environment in which they grow up. Yes, there is discipline alongside guidance. Of course, at this age, there are many—in fact, most—decisions we still make for our kids, but at the ripe age of six and eight, I am already finding that our world gives them responsibilities. It teaches them to be independent and gives them the opportunity to make their own decisions and mistakes.

Perhaps they will grow up feeling like their Asian father was particularly *Asian* in his style of parenting, perhaps they will see me as strict, perhaps unreasonable at times. Perhaps it will be the opposite, and they'll wonder why we didn't discipline them harder, like some of their local friends! But I will continue to do my best for them; I will continue to uphold our family values, while showing them a deep and unconditional love. I may—no, I definitely will—fail every now and again, but I guess this is the journey of life, particularly parenthood. My hope is that the foundations we lay in our children are strong enough to help them weather the storms of life. I hope we teach them to love. I hope we show them that they are loved.

Chapter 8

More than Just a Helper

Sometimes at work, or in life, we are given a position or a title. It's amazing how we often find identity in that title—perhaps it's the power we are seen to have, or a significant position, or even our value as an employee, volunteer or even as a leader. It was my 23rd or perhaps 24th birthday. My very good friend and housemate, Phil, had recently graduated as a medical doctor after five years of study and he took me out to buy me a present to celebrate. We were in the Chapelfield Shopping Centre in Norwich where we lived at the time—we had both gone to university there and had both decided to make Norwich our home. I picked out a really nice-looking pair of boots—leather, brown, army style boots—an "in" style at the time. I tried them on and they fitted perfectly, so we took them to the counter for Phil to pay. The shop assistant behind the counter looked at our fresh faces and said to Phil, "Spending our student loan, are we?"

"No, I'm a doctor," came a stern but clear response. Of course, I found this profoundly funny, and went on to do some of my finest impressions as we left the shop, and again when we met up with some friends later that day. We still joke about it today and I think I have honed my impressionist skills almost to perfection!

Phil would respond with, "I didn't study medicine for five years to be called a student!" And he had a point. We all appreciate a good title, or recognition for our efforts. I love seeing newly qualified teachers writing their name on their planners as "Miss Humphries" or "Mr King" There is a pride in their achievement, a pride in their roles—and rightly so.

I understand it is this same pride that caused a fracture in the relationship between my family and the lady who was our live-in helper for six wonderful years. Lita played a hugely important role in my life. While my father was studying hard at his masters and my mother was working solidly to provide for our family, Lita took on the role of my parent. She fed me, washed me, played with me and loved me. I remember her getting us ready in the mornings and getting us set for bed in the evenings. I remember her holding my chin as she brushed my teeth. To my parents, she was a part of our family. She was their employee, yes, but I never felt like she was just that, and nor did they.

We stayed in touch with Lita after she left to go and live in Canada. Every now and again we would buy an international calling card—a card that provided us with a certain amount of minutes to call abroad at a discounted price—and call Lita for a catch up. It's strange to think that these days, a video call can be made for free at any time of the day, no matter where we are. One day she called and we all had a chance to catch up. The house we lived in at the time had a wireless telephone that sat on a sideboard in the hallway—the same sideboard that once kept all of our home videos in its lowest drawer. We would sit on the stairs and talk on the phone, as, despite its wireless capabilities, we still needed to be within a certain proximity of the receiver. My younger sister, Amanda, had finished her conversation with Lita and was ready to pass the phone onto my parents to wrap up the call. She had a friend over that day who asked who was on the phone. Amanda's innocent response hurt Lita. "It's our old maid," she replied.

Amanda's feelings and association with the word "maid" was only one of respect and love. It was never meant as derogatory or lacking in value, but it hurt Lita and made her feel devalued. She saw the terms *helper* or *nanny* of far more worth than *maid*. In Canada, she was referred to as a governess, a position which came with the gravitas of running a home. It was this one word and its perceived meaning that caused Lita to withdraw from our family. That was the last phone call we had with her, my grandparents remaining in touch for a few more years before we lost all communication.

In Singapore, helpers would normally eat at a different time to the rest of the family, or eat in the kitchen, away from the family. They would often live in a separate area, designed and built closer to the kitchen and away from the rest of the home. It is easy for a helper to be inconspicuous and even invisible.

In 2018, my family and I were on the receiving end of some incredible generosity from friends of my parents, who gave us their apartment to stay in for our Christmas holiday, since they were travelling abroad. Their home was beautiful. The taxi drove into the basement car park and dropped us off at the lift lobby, where we had a special credit-card sized key fob to let us into the lift. This seems to be fairly standard in condos in

Singapore. We piled our bags into the lift: one big red suitcase, one bright orange duffle bag, a couple of backpacks and two mini-suitcases that our children had filled with books and toys. One floor up—a ground-level apartment. The lift doors opened, directly into their apartment! We dragged our things in and looked around the beautiful home. It was spacious. The ceilings were high. Glass double doors separated the kitchen and the open-plan living area and dining room. Our gratitude was accompanied by amazement at this beautiful home— and it was ours for the holidays. Next to the living room was another set of sliding doors, leading to a terrace, which led to the pool area. There were some beautiful plants and paved walkways, too.

We settled into the apartment and to our surprise, the family's helper was there to help us with anything we needed. She was friendly, with long, black, straight hair that reached her lower back. Our children took a shine to her, but she was careful to keep her distance. Our children are very used to trusting the people in our home and I think the separation intrigued them. The following morning she asked if we wanted anything to drink and we let her know that we were happy to help ourselves; but we became aware that by trying to do anything ourselves made her feel very awkward. That morning I had asked for coffee, but it turns out our hosts were not coffee drinkers, so I settled for some fruit juice instead. The next morning she had bought coffee and had it brewing ready for when we emerged from our slumber. My only experience of a helper was Lita, and I found it very foreign to be waited upon like this.

In our last few days, out of gratitude to her, we invited her to join us for a walk and picnic around the Singapore Botanic Gardens. The Botanic Gardens is a UNESCO World Heritage Site, with stunning plants and trees, but also some great spots for kids to play. She agreed to join us. It was late morning and so we decided to stop at a hawker centre for some early lunch. We first noticed that the helper wouldn't walk with us—she remained a few paces behind. Millie tried to have some conversation with her and she was happy to answer, but from a distance. We tried slowing down, to give her a chance to catch up, but she slowed down too. At the hawker centre, she wouldn't sit at the table with us, despite our invitation, and even our insistence. When we got to the Botanic Gardens, she didn't want to sit at the same bench as us and we realised that she simply felt awkward about it— and our constant encouragement to do so made her feel even more uncomfortable. So we stopped insisting. But then *we* felt uncomfortable. It was a very strange exchange of awkwardness, but we eventually understood that gaining an understanding or relationship with this lady would take time and trust. Later, on relaying this with my parents, they were not surprised at all and had to explain to me that Lita, our helper from my childhood, was exactly the same, that it took a lot of time for her to feel welcome at the family table.

Lita joined us for family holidays, as a part of the family, and she enjoyed weekends with us, too. I remember the big freeze of 1987—I wasn't even three years old, so I remember it through our family videos. We wrapped up warm and made our way out into our little garden to explore the snow. It was my first experience of snow, having lived in Singapore up until this point. I was in a little grey coat and I wore mittens that were attached to each other by a long piece of wool that was threaded up one sleeve, across the inside of my coat and down the other sleeve. Now that I think of it, I wonder why we didn't do this for my own children when we lived in the UK. It would certainly have saved a few pounds and would have reduced the number of solo gloves in our hats-and-gloves basket. Lita wore a woolly hat. The family video has a clip of my mother, gloves on her hands, trying to put my older sister's hat on for her, but accidentally covering her eyes! Lita had not experienced snow before either and the joy, excitement and wonder was visible. The snow cover was deep—nearly two foot—as we clambered over the top, sinking with every step into the dry and powdery snow. We decided to build some snowmen. My dad helped us build one. It was a huge mound of snow that we piled together using a dustbin lid, scooping and dragging the dusty ice into a pile. We made a face and wrapped a scarf around it. Lita took a lot of care and attention over her snowman, shaping the head perfectly before pushing into her own, much smaller snow pile. She laughed so much, real joy bubbling up. She was still shy, covering her mouth as she laughed.

The day Lita left remains vivid in my mind. I was six years old. I don't remember the build-up, or how my parents told me she was going to leave us. I don't even know the reasons for her departure and the timing of it—whether my parents could no longer afford her, whether she felt it was time to move on, or whether, with my sisters and I being that bit older, we didn't need her anymore. I don't remember the journey to the airport, or checking in her bags. I don't know whether we stopped for food before she left. But one of the clearest memories of my childhood was watching her walk through the gates at the departures area of Heathrow Airport in London. I remember balling my eyes out, crying loudly as she left. Strangely, I can still remember how the pain felt. If I close my eyes and place myself there, the feeling of loss still aches in the pit of my stomach. It is strange, as it has been 30 years now—but I guess that goes to show what a significant impact that separation had on my life. Recently, I shared these thoughts with my parents. It seems my reaction to saying goodbye was one that stuck with them, too. My mother remembers taking me to the Disney store and buying a couple of movies on VHS for us to take home and watch. I still find comfort in the old Disney movies.

I only saw Lita one more time after she left. She came to visit with her husband, a Canadian-German named Stefan, when I was about 10 or 11 years old. He seemed friendly—he had white hair and wore glasses. She seemed different that day, but I can't describe how. I sat next to her on the sofa, perhaps slightly awkwardly. I don't remember them leaving.

In my early 20s, going through teacher training, I learned a lot about trauma in children and the difficulties children can experience in separation. It was strange, yet enlightening to be able to trace many of my own insecurities and mental struggles to that point of separation. It was an interesting time for internal processing and I found it helpful to be able to explain my own insecurities and to be more aware of triggers for my mental health. For example, when I was 16, my older sister, Charmaine, went to Spain for part of her gap year—a year of experiencing the world before she went to university. I remember feeling incredibly low—depressed, even. One dinner time, I broke down and cried, sobbed. Now looking back, I realise this was my first time experiencing loss or separation since Lita left. I didn't realise this back then, I just knew that I felt uncontrollably low. It's amazing how much easier it is now knowing there was a simple explanation for that feeling.

***

In 2013, my younger sister Amanda went to live in Singapore with her husband and son. Her experience of living in Singapore was far different to the homecoming that I felt. My older sister, Charmaine, considers Singapore to be a bit more like one's parents' home. It is familiar and feels comforting to be there, but you know you live somewhere else. These vast differences in experiences and feelings forced me to examine why we should respond so differently to being in Singapore. Both Charmaine and Amanda were born in the UK, and Charmaine lived in Singapore from ages 1–5, attending local kindergarten, too. Amanda grew up in the UK, never having lived in Singapore. As siblings, our family environment was the same, our family culture was the same.

The only significant contrast is that I had Lita as my own helper from birth until age six. It made me wonder whether her personal style, mannerisms, demeanour—her personal culture—was one that had a particularly large influence on me. I wonder how much impact her Filipino culture had on me. There are many migrant domestic workers in Singapore, supporting families just as mine was supported. Most of these hail from the Philippines and Indonesia and I wonder how much of their culture is absorbed by the children whom they support. How much of the Singaporean culture is influenced by these women, who are often working away from their own children to be able to earn and send money home? The past two years have featured a drastic limit in air travel and so we haven't been able to visit the Philippines, as was our plan. I would have loved the opportunity to go and see how much of Lita's culture rubbed off on me, and to see how much of the Filipino culture has either influenced Singapore's—or at least how much of it is similar.

I began paying closer attention to my friends and acquaintances from the Philippines and I found I was unintentionally asking more questions about their home country, culture and daily life. I discovered that my friends from the big cities, like Manila, had a very different life to Lita. She came from a village and life there seemed to be quite rural. I didn't have any details, just a story or two from Stefan on that day they visited us. One of my Filipino friends works in a café in Singapore. One day, we got talking and I found myself asking about her home. She described waking up early to feed her goats and chickens, the open spaces of greenery and a large home. I tried to picture Lita in that setting, but struggled to connect my own story to this context.

I spoke with Filipino lawyers, teachers, nurses, baristas, students and helpers—just like Lita. They all, of course, had their own personalities, some shy, some outgoing, some loud, some quiet. All of the Filipino people I spoke to had the same warmth that Lita did, even the new friends. They had an immediate sense of kindness: a compliment, a smile, encouragement. None of it was forced or disingenuous. This warmth was something I definitely remember being an attribute of Lita's and it seems to be cultural, as well as personal. When the skies reopen and global travel recommences, I would love the opportunity to visit the Philippines and experience the local people, flavours, sites and communities for myself. The warmth of the Filipino people is different to that of Singaporeans. Singaporeans are a little more guarded—incredibly warm with those they know, but reserved with strangers. Perhaps this trait has not been passed on. It may have been a stretch to assume that Filipino helpers pass on their kindness and cheerfulness to Singaporeans, since they have an employee–employer relationship, although I am sure they have an influence in many less obvious ways.

On watching interactions between helpers and children, particularly in the homes of our friends, most helpers have a different relationship with their families to the one we had with Lita. As I mentioned, most apartments or houses have a room and bathroom dedicated to the use of a helper. Ours is the other side of our kitchen, but we don't have a helper at home, so the room doubles up as storage for skateboards, scooters and Christmas decorations. There is a clear separation between family and helper. From my observations I can see that the roles are closer to employer–employee, rather than an extended family member.

***

I must have felt that looking for Lita was a lost cause—my mother couldn't remember her new surname, my grandparents no longer knew her address. I had Google searched her full name a few times, adding "Canada" to the search bar, hoping something would come up. She must be in her mid-60s now. I also had to combat a few internal thoughts and emotions. My parents are wonderful people and have been consistently loving and caring parents since day one. I wouldn't want them to feel I had a need to find Lita—this lady who I feel was like a parent to me for my first six years. They are totally sufficient for me. I also wasn't sure what emotions I would feel. A 37-year-old man, searching out a lady in her 60s to reunite—it seemed a bit strange at times. But for some reason, one cool and breezy Singapore day, I decided that I would try again to look for her.

I sent my parents a message on our WhatsApp group: "Do either of you remember Lita's new surname, or her husband's name?"

The same response came from my mother that I had a few years before: "Sorry darling, I don't remember his surname, but his first name was Stefan." Ah yes, I had remembered that first name. But there must have been hundreds of Stefans living in Canada.

My internet search changed. "Stefan and Lita, Canada." Come on, Google, you can do this, bring me the results I need… a string of unrelated content appeared. I clicked on a few, hoping something would connect some dots, but nothing.

That's when my phone buzzed with a message from my father. "Their surname is Meyer."

Quickly, I searched Facebook, Instagram, Twitter... nothing came up. Google brought up one name on a Canadian directory, a simple S. Meyer, addressed to Ontario, Canada and a number. I picked up my phone and dialled.

"The number you have dialled has not been recognised. Please check and try again", came the pre-recorded lady's voice. I checked it—I had dialled exactly what was listed. In blind hope, I tried again, same number, hoping for a different result. "The number you have dialled has not been recognised." Back to square one. I tried messaging my friend, Ben, who joined me for some of my pilgrimage around Singapore, as he had recently moved back to Canada. He didn't respond, so I went back to an internet search.

Finally, one evening, I decided for some strange reason to check YouTube. I sat in our study at home. I turned on the computer, opened the internet and typed into the search bar, "Stefan Meyer". There were a few of them. I clicked on one. Three videos, two subscribers. One video was of some children singing Christmas songs in a Filipino village. The place looked rural, like the sort Stefan had described. It had been uploaded in 2012, and then there were two more videos, uploaded in 2021! I clicked on them—they were both reviews of some computer hardware. I listened intently—a soft German accent, perhaps a bit of Canadian too, but there was no footage of his face. I suddenly caught a glimpse of his face in a reflection in the video: white hair, glasses. Could it be a coincidence? This man, the right sort of age, with white hair and glasses, the same name and with a video from a Filipino village—surely this was him. I frantically search for an email address, but found nothing. So I wrote a comment, "Is this the same Stefan Meyer who married Lita? I'm trying to get in touch with her." I pressed enter and waited.

I worked out what time it was in Canada. Only 8pm. There must be time, I'm sure he'd check it. I waited, refreshed the page and waited again. Over the following few days I went back to check whether he had read my message, but there was no response. I tried the same number on the phone again, but nothing.

***

As time has passed, I have had a chance to process my thoughts, and more importantly, my heartfelt feelings. It has become clearer to me that there is still a feeling of curiosity, perhaps even a sense of loss that I have not yet settled with regards to Lita. In this journey and personal exploration, I have reopened an area of my childhood that has remained closed for the best part of three decades. Rather than a reopening, perhaps of a box or a chest, it has been more like picking at an old scab— the hard protective, thick skin, peeled back and a raw, slightly messy, unhealed wound has been exposed. I had hoped to find that her significance in my life provided insight into my sense of belonging in Singapore, or perhaps in Asia. But I don't think this is the case. While Lita had a significant place in my life and early development, I'm not sure that this is the same story across all families in Singapore.

In closing this chapter, I do so with few conclusions, and maybe more questions. It is important and healthy to note that my feelings of discomfort are valid—separation from a significant adult at a young age can have a lasting impact. Lita was a source of provision, protection and love. Perhaps this is a pain to bear, perhaps the peeling of this scab is a chance for it to heal properly. Perhaps it is the start of another story of reconnection, restoration and reunion. I guess only time will tell.

Chapter 9

Going Deeper

The vast majority of my journey has been a personal investigation into my emotions and thoughts, my understanding of Singapore and my understanding of self. At times I have considered my own story a case study in a "Third Culture Kid", learning about my experiences and even applying some of these thoughts to students who I encounter at work. I believe my deepened understandings have allowed me to become a better teacher, a more supportive mentor and a more compassionate person. Many of my experiences and findings have been anecdotal and I wanted to know if science could back up some of my findings and more importantly, I wondered whether it could reveal more.

Over the years, my family often speculated that we must have had some Portuguese DNA in our system. One year we all went to Melaka in Malaysia for a holiday. We drove from Singapore and we stayed in some chalets on the beach. I'm not sure how accurate my memories are from that time. In my mind I can see a play park and fencing around our chalets, the sea lapping in the distance. We went into the city for a meal one evening with my Uncle Charles and Auntie Maureen. We ate outside. Countless stray cats were meandering around us, looking for a bite to eat.

There were cats climbing on the tables of the customers who had just left, tucking into the remaining food. I wasn't convinced of the cleanliness of the red plastic table cloths, even after the waiter wiped it down.

Melaka is an old port town on the western coast of Malaysia. It's where Grandpa was born and where we assume his roots are from. On that trip with my family, my parents stumbled upon a community of people, all with very similar features to Grandpa. Wavy, almost curly hair, rounder eyes, darker skin. This community were descendants of the Portuguese who had settled in Malaysia. It really seemed likely he belonged there and we were convinced this was the case, so much so that I even claimed that I was "probably somewhere between an eighth and sixteenth Portuguese", even without any other evidence.

My journey of self-discovery and the questions I was regularly asking my parents caught my father's attention and he decided to get a DNA test to find out, once and for all, whether there was any European blood in our ancestry line. We were pretty adamant that my mother was a thoroughbred Chinese, with her parents hailing from mainland China. My father's parents, though, had histories shrouded in mystery. We knew very little of my grandpa's history—his father did not look Chinese at all, in fact he looked quite western. Grandma had been adopted twice, first by a lady, second by the lady's lover and his family— the makings of a gripping drama. Perhaps that's why she loved watching soap operas, tuning in religiously every night.

My parents were in Singapore on holiday, visiting us, when my father's DNA results came through. He emailed a link to me and my sisters. I opened the link and scanned the peoples represented in his DNA. To my huge surprise, I saw that just two per cent of my father's DNA was of this region—Singapore, Indonesia, Malaysia, Myanmar, Brunei. I was amazed how the whole region was sectioned off into one group. To me, it seemed like a very wide net for a very diverse region. However, this region was historically so closely connected through trade—spices and produce were not the only things that were shared across the seas, but people, too—and people moved around and settled in different parts of this region. I find it amazing how I can often have dinner with local friends and around the table we have people from Malaysia, Indonesia, Burma. We are a truly blended region.

The next 7 per cent of DNA was attributed to Vietnam. This was a very interesting find as we had no idea of any Vietnamese blood in the family. However, with my grandma being adopted a couple of times, we do not have any clues as to her ancestry. If this DNA came from her side of the family, I would love to know the details of her journey or the journey of her biological parents. All we know is that she was an orphan in Singapore in the early 1930s.

The final chunk of DNA was the most compelling: 91 per cent from southern China. None from Portugal, not even any DNA of the Dutch settlers in the region either—in fact, nothing from Europe at all. What I found most strange was my response to this finding. For so long, I had hoped that I had a smidgen, even 1 per cent of European blood. I thought that these findings would be a disappointment to me, but instead, it felt fine. It felt good actually. I realised at that point, my insecurities about where I belonged had gone. I think they had been gone for a while, but there was a freedom I had not paid attention to before. I was happy with where I was from—it made sense. My feeling of home fitted my DNA, now knowing my father's genetic make-up confirmed that I was where I was supposed to be. I was happy to be living in that area, feeling like I was home. No European DNA, but fully Asian.

***

My first year of university life was in Northampton, a rather dingy town in the East Midlands of England. It was my first real taste of freedom and I loved my final two months living there. Exams were over and for some reason I still had time remaining on the lease of my room, so we spent about eight glorious weeks living it up, partying into the night until the sun rose in the early hours. I decided that this life of partying was the way I wanted to go and so when I transferred university at the end of the year, I decided to choose the cheapest student accommodation I could find. Waveney Terrace was already an infamous block at the University of East Anglia, in the beautiful city of Norwich. Rumoured to have been modelled on a prison, this self-catered accommodation boasted 14 rooms and a kitchen-dining room that seated four people around an aluminium table. The aluminium sides of the kitchen prep surfaces would become too hot to touch when the oven was left on. Along the hallway from the kitchen were three toilet cubicles and two showers, which we all shared. Waveney Terrace was known as the cheap 'n' nasty rooms that only party-heads would sleep in, and I had the privilege of staying there in its final year of existence. To be clear: many blocks had already been demolished in the summer before I arrived and only a handful of blocks were still in function. We were not asked to lay a deposit for any damages to the rooms as a result, and so things got broken pretty quickly. Our toilet doors and shower curtains got stolen by another flat a few floors above us and so we were forced to become comfortable with each other quite quickly. We tried to give them a bit of payback by padlocking their fridge and cutting the wire to the plug. We could smell the rotting food in their third-floor kitchen all the way down in our ground floor rooms.

Half way through my first year in Norwich, someone took advantage of the broken lock on my window, popped into my room while I was out one day and departed with my laptop. I hadn't backed up any of my assignments and I was due to hand in some important and significant projects two weeks later. This unfortunate incident (and my lack of backing up) resulted in me making the difficult decision to postpone the rest of my year's studies until the next academic year. It was around this time that I began to rediscover my Christian faith, which probably came at the perfect time as my lifestyle was becoming pretty destructive, with drinking and partying among some of my priorities.

It was springtime in 2006 when two lads from church invited me to move into a room in their house. Little did I know, these lads would become among the best friends I have ever had— Owen and Phil. Owen had recently graduated from university and was working in a nearby department store selling barista coffee machines, while Phil was in his fourth year of medical school. Over the years our friendships have grown. We have navigated many seasons together, been groomsmen at each others' weddings and, even now, in three different cities across the world, are still in each others' lives.

After many more years of studying, Phil qualified as a psychiatrist. He would often joke about analysing us and digging up our past, which is funny because I asked him to do exactly that regarding my journey of self-discovery. While the DNA tests gave me a biological understanding of my make-up, I was keen to see whether any certain events or elements of my childhood, both in Singapore and the UK, were significant in my understanding of home, now, as an adult.

Phil has a massive flaw. Irritatingly, it is also one of his great strengths. He is always late. It is a strength because the reason why he is late is that he is a diligent worker and a relentlessly loyal friend—if he feels someone needs more time, he will give them more time. With the time difference between Singapore and the UK, I had a quick nap and set up my laptop for a late-night call with Phil. With 10 minutes to go, I dropped him a message just to remind him and check that he was set.

"I'm afraid I'm running a bit behind," came the reply.

"How late? What sort of time works for you?" I hoped Phil could feel my slight irritation through his phone screen.

"Would tomorrow work better for you?" he responded. "I'm just organising a load of things for the arrival of our baby."

I felt guilty for being annoyed. He was approaching fatherhood for the first time. Eventually we decided on a phone call to decide when we could do the real interview. I couldn't help but feel a bit put out, but I knew Phil was often late, I just forgot as we hadn't lived in the same city for a few years.

So we had a quality catch-up with conversation mainly centred around Phil soon becoming a father and then we got into the nitty gritty. He then asked me heaps of questions, almost like a background check, before we had a proper discussion about the things that caused me to feel at home in Singapore. We went through some of the journey I had been on since 2014 and assessed a few of the things that I had managed to conclude from my life. He asked me about significant moments, but didn't ask too much detail. Eventually, we called it a night and decided the next day would be the official interview.

I'm not sure what I was hoping to find out from Phil in that interview. I wondered if these complex situations and experiences of my childhood in some way caused me to feel more at home in Singapore than in England. I knew that, while Phil didn't specialise in this aspect of psychiatry, his expertise plus our relationship meant that he had an insight about me and the freedom to ask me anything he wanted with the knowledge that I would answer him honestly and openly. Phil asked me about early memories. I relayed stories of my fourth birthday, throwing my pacifier in the bin. I told him about Lita, the day she left and about that horrible journey to school with my grandpa a couple of years later.

"That's really interesting," he said in response to the account. "Your grandfather saying he didn't love you was like the loss of someone close to you."

"What do you mean?" I ask, a little puzzled.

"Well, the only thing to which your eight-year-old mind could compare the pain of your grandpa saying he didn't love you was the passing away of your family pet."

I hadn't ever seen it that way. I knew it was a painful experience and that the fallout of it lasted a while, but being able to put it into context of loss made so much sense. I wonder if that displacement of love or affection from my Peranakan heritage added to my desire to find it, to embrace it and ultimately, to be accepted by it? Returning to Singapore on holiday in 2014, I felt at home—perhaps subconsciously, I felt like I was finally accepted. A lifetime of carrying this hurt may have been resolved in Singapore being welcoming, safe, fun and secure—all feelings I had longed for as a result of the fractured relationship between my grandfather and me. If eight-year-old me felt such an overwhelming loss, perhaps this explains why adult me felt so "found".

Phil went on to explain how this experience as well as the loss of Lita at a young age has clearly played a huge part in my desire for love in my life and the way I am emotionally moved in times of extreme love or loss. On a negative side, this left me as an insecure teenager into my early 20s—insecurities that, I believe, were only helped by my Christian faith. My insecurities meant that I must have been a nightmare to date, constantly looking for affection, security and reassurance from women and constantly doing things for the attention of my mates and for their approval. While some of these times have provided me with good memories, I can see and acknowledge where much of my motivation behind behaviours was unhealthy and unhelpful to me and some of those around me. I hurt a lot of people going from relationship to relationship. I caused a lot of trouble seeking the attention of my peers.

The other aspect is one that I have embraced. I wear my heart on my sleeve and I am moved to action when I see a lack of love. I am moved to tears when I see an abundance of love. I can scroll through the news and well up with tears of sadness as I read about another missing child, or another murder. Tears of joy roll down my face when I see someone go out of their way to be kind to someone in need. I even cry at Disney movies! As Phil spoke, I could see pieces of the puzzle of my life fitting together. Not to say that I felt puzzled, but each piece that I had previously known had been fitted into its context and it created a wider perspective and a greater understanding of myself.

My secure home and loving parents have contributed to the huge value I place on family. Singapore also places value on family—so much so, that in many instances, I have seen the public in Singapore act like a big family. It is worth mentioning again the safety of Singapore's streets and public spaces. It is so safe, I have noticed a level of comfort—or perhaps even complacency. We were at a food court having a drink recently, my father, Milo and me, and Milo said he needed to go to the washroom. He said I didn't need to accompany him, that he knew where it was. Firstly, an eight-year-old kid was happy to go unaccompanied to the washroom, which was a good 50 metres away. I love that he already felt safe enough to be able to do that. After checking with him a few times that he was confident with where to go, off he went. My father and I got chatting over our *kopi* and *teh*, and before I knew it, 10 minutes had passed. It felt like a long time, but again, I considered the option that he needed to do… something more substantial on his visit to the washroom, so I waited a bit longer. Two or three minutes later he showed up, looking a bit sheepish.

"I got a bit lost on my way back", Milo said with a grin on his face.

"You wally," I responded, ruffling his overgrown hair, "Just come back the way you came!"

We had a good chuckle about it all and then thought nothing more of it. This sense of security and home is one that any parent would want for their children, right? I am aware that crime does still happen in Singapore and that people can still do unkind and unlawful things, and so I think I need to be more careful as a parent, but this sense of safety is healthy.

During our holiday in Singapore in 2014, we went to a food court one afternoon for lunch. My grandparents were with us, and as normal, my grandma would shuffle off looking for her pick of the day. She came back to our table with no food and sat down. "Are you OK, Grandma? You don't want to eat?"

"Tsst. Of course—the boy is bringing my food for me." She replied, slightly dismissively, but still gentle and loving in a way only Grandma can. She waved her hand in the direction of the stall where she bought her food and there I saw a teenage lad carrying Grandma's meal for her. He was a member of the public, stood in the line behind her and had insisted he helped her with her meal.

"Here, aunty," he said as he placed the tray down on the table. "Careful, it's hot."

I was amazed. I asked Grandma if she knew him, or his parents, but she insisted this happens regularly and that the boy was just being helpful. Too focused on my own meal, I hadn't even thought about helping her, yet, in Singapore, teenagers went out of their way to help the elderly. I felt challenged and I learned so much from that one interaction. This big-family-feeling across the country is one I still feel regularly in Singapore. It has been hindered a little by COVID-19 and the precautions people take, but it is still there. I know many Singaporeans feel that this sense of community—or the *kampong* spirit—is dying out, but I sincerely hope it doesn't, and I am committed to doing my part to ensure it remains.

I enjoyed the way Phil asked me very simple questions that required in-depth responses. I had to think to be able to articulate. I was being forced to discover, but all of the discoveries were already in my own head—he just helped me to draw them out and identify and categorise them. I learned that I enjoyed feeling part of the crowd in Singapore. I could put on a pair of shorts and a t-shirt, wander out into the streets and there was nothing distinctive about me. I didn't realise how much I felt like I stood out in the UK, as someone with oriental features. I always felt foreign, even in the country I grew up in, where I lived for 34 years. I just didn't realise it until I compared with how comfortable I felt in Singapore. Perhaps if this realisation came sooner, I could have embraced being *the Foreign Local,* rather than *the Local Immigrant.* But there were many other things that led to my feeling of home.

Chapter 10

Reunion

It was a fairly normal morning, the warmth of the day had already started to break through and it was only 7am. I walked out of the air-conditioned MRT station, down the hill to my school—sweat already starting to collect under my face mask. I wished all of the school security guards a good morning and they, as ever, wished me a good morning back—happy, grateful people. I got into the elevator, the *beep* of the buttons, silent to me, as I was listening to music through some earphones. I walked into my office, turned on the light and the air-con, sat down and opened my laptop.

After answering some emails and getting my lessons set for the day, I spotted I had a notification from my personal email account. I clicked on it and saw a message from YouTube. "S. Meyer has replied to your comment." I quickly opened a new tab in my internet browser, typed in YouTube.com and went to the video.

"What's your interest in getting to know me?" read the reply. Hmm. No acknowledgement of me being wrong about who this was, but no confirmation that I was right, either. I suddenly became aware that my heart was beating hard and that I was feeling a little nervous. Had I found Stefan? I replied quickly, explaining who I was and that I was hoping to be in touch with Lita. So many scenarios went through my mind. Why did he not mention Lita? Was she OK? Were they still together? What if she didn't want to hear from me? Was she even still alive? To be honest, I still wasn't really sure of my exact reason for wanting to get in touch—I just knew I wanted to speak to her, or just to reach out and see how she was doing.

A few days later I received a reply. "That's very nice of you. What's your email address?" This time, I felt there was a little more confirmation that I had found him—hopefully *them*—but I still wasn't too sure. We eventually connected via email, a wonderful reply from Stefan that confirmed Lita was indeed alive, well and wondering how I was and what I looked like. "It is 10.43pm, and so we are off to bed. I will email you in the morning."

I had found her. Years of lost contact all made well with a short and simple email. I felt happy, calm. I had expected more, perhaps—more emotion—but I was content.

A couple of hours later, I had just come out of a meeting at work and my phone buzzed. An email notification, from Emelita Meyer, subject heading: "Memories, our picture 1986 to 1987". I quickly walked down to my office, shut the door and opened my laptop. I was excited—Lita had stayed up an extra two hours, maybe thinking about me and how I was. It was half past midnight in Canada. I clicked on the email—a lovely personal message. She signed off with, "You were a very cute and very good boy." Attached was an image. Double click. It opened. Not just a picture of us, but several pictures, cut out in scrap-book style, clearly treasured for more than 30 years.

I welled up. The emotion that I was expecting in that first contact suddenly came not as a wave but more like a tsunami. I tried my hardest to hold it back—I was at work, and my office was divided from the hallway by a glass partition, where students would be passing by any minute now. I closed my eyes—held them shut. A tear escaped, but got caught between my nose and cheek. A deep breath. Another deep breath.

That evening somehow I got home before Millie and the kids. I think they detoured or something. The kids got home and I was sitting at the dining table, a beautiful Peranakan tiled table that I'm sure will become an heirloom in the years to come. I turned around at the delightful sound of Aspen shouting "Daddy!", one of the best sounds a father can hear. I gave the kids a big hug, bigger than normal—I appreciated our bond all the more that day. Milo and Aspen went off to play in Aspen's room for a while, a rare silence descending upon a full house.

"How was your day, love?" Millie asked. This routine question was never insincere, always asked with care and interest.

"I actually have a lot to share with you today," I replied. I twisted around on our dining bench to face her as she sat on a couch. "I heard from Lita today."

A smile came to my face, a strange grimace made by the tension between joy and holding back joyful tears. I relayed the story of my day to her and read the emails, even the comments I made on Stefan's YouTube channel. I hadn't updated Millie for a while as I was pretty sure that no results would come of my search. As I read, I came to the part where Lita sent me some photos. I walked over to the couch and sat next to Millie. She came in close as I opened the photo on my phone. "You see, she has treasured these scrapbook cut-outs, I think she must have thought of me as much as I have of her." Millie's head was resting on my shoulder, providing a comfort that only she can. I got a glimpse of her cheeks. Tears were making their way down her face too, like a ski slalom, rolling slowly over the contours of the dimple that graces just one cheek. Millie doesn't often cry. Strangely, in Millie's tears I saw what it meant to her, but also what this reconnection meant to me. Despite usually wearing my heart on my sleeve, I think I had tried to avoid feeling too much about this situation, as I thought finding Lita was unlikely to happen. Millie is an amazing wife. She knows me better than I know myself and in that moment, she showed me how much weight she had carried in this search, too. She felt it all: the separation, the tension, the reunion.

As weeks went by we sent email after email, photo after photo, catching up on the past 30 years. The first photo I sent her of Milo she replied: "Your boy looks just like you—really, exactly the same! I thought it was you!" I am so grateful to be back in touch with Lita and I hope to be able to visit her in the coming years with my family.

Chapter 11

Makan

Grandma had a shuffle and a waddle as she walked, her hands soft, delicate, gripping my forearm for extra balance and support. She was very small, with a cute nose that held up her glasses. Her silver hair was smooth and straight, like silk curtains that sat perfectly above her shoulders. Grandma made her own dresses, a skill that I guess she developed when she was posted overseas, away from Grandpa, who remained in Singapore—a way of occupying her time in the age before social media and the internet. She had found the dress shape and size that she liked and then stuck to it, changing just the fabric each time—each floral-patterned dress a clone of the last.

Grandpa and Grandma would ask, weeks in advance, for our flight details: date, flight number, arrival time, arrival terminal. When I was in my late teens, my grandparents moved back to Singapore. At the time they were in their early 70s and I guess they wanted to be back home. On our visits back to Singapore, my grandparents would always meet us at the arrivals gate, and we'd go and eat at the food court in the airport before we went on to wherever we were going to stay—usually at either Uncle Robin and Auntie Lorraine's (one of my mother's older sisters) or at Uncle Adrian and Auntie Shook Wah's. Auntie Shook Wah was not a blood-aunt, although there was a distant familial connection. Her brother married one of my mother's sisters.

In the weeks leading up to each family holiday in Singapore, conversations around our own dinner table would be punctuated with what we were looking forward to eating when we arrived. As I got older, I would return to the cloudy and grey UK with the sunny island still in my heart and began trying to recreate my favourite dishes. Bee hoon was an easy one, and it was popular with my mates at university, too. After the abuse with which we'd treated it, our accommodation had become disgusting: the carpets were sticky from years of not being cleaned properly. I remember one evening a plate of bee hoon ended up on the floor, but was still eaten by my flatmates and me. Either the food was good or the times were hard. Perhaps both.

When Millie and I first met, she only really enjoyed food the English way—boiled, baked and bland. She'd probably disagree that the food was wholly bland and she'd probably be right. But there was a lack of variety, for sure. Slowly I introduced her to spices, seafood, tropical fruits… flavour! She was a convert with every bite. She would help me make dishes for our friends and she learned recipes from my mother, too. One of her favourites is lor bak, a braised belly pork with a feast of spices and dark soy. One time we made nasi lemak for some friends—we even dried shrimp to make the sambal and fried chicken wings in batter. Some of the favourite dishes and foods we made were curry puffs, bak kut teh, beef rendang, laksa and chicken rice.

Before long, Millie and I got married and with the birth of Milo, we decided it was time to visit the motherland. That was her first visit, back in 2014. The flight was also Millie's first long-haul flight and Milo had just turned one. His cheeks became all rosy while we were in the air. The flight attendants were smitten with Milo: his big, round marble-like eyes, chubby cheeks and his love for life was irresistible and they scooped him up and played with him at every opportunity they could. He even got a ride around the aisles on an empty food cart.

We landed at Changi Airport and before we could even emerge from the aircon and feel the familiar warm, tropical air enter our lungs, we were met by Grandma and Grandpa, who led us to the food court—a branch of the Kopitiam chain. I was ready to spend a few saved dollars from my previous trip—neatly folded in my wallet as a reminder of my holidays past and of my holiday to come. Each time I opened my wallet, I would dream of my next return—it even added to my discipline to save money for our flights. I remember imagining spending those dollars at that Kopitiam, char kway teow (my favourite dish) being tossed around the wok, flames bursting over the edge every now and again. I could smell it—dark, smokey.

Grandma held onto my arm as I pushed our trolley of luggage. She asked me not to get any more tattoos and I had to convince her I was not in a gang. Meeting my son, her great-grandson, for the first time, distracted her from the cross examination and she and my Grandpa held him with pride. Great-grandchild number four. We made our way to the food court and I remember feeling hungry and being very aware of the pace, or lack thereof, that we were maintaining—Grandma slowing down in her old age. By then, she was already in her late 80s.

At times over the years there would be a small entourage of family with us, too. The largest I can remember was 16 of us. It must have been quite a sight for anyone looking on, a huge family descending upon the food court and a tiny old lady bossing everyone around. She would always be so determined to *chope* (reserve) a set of tables all together, and to seat 16 people plus luggage took some skill among fierce competition. Millie had become an adventurous eater and went off in her own hunt for new flavours. I took my time. Slowly, I walked around all of the stalls, taking in all of the options, scanning both dishes as well as prices in a pre-meal ritual, before settling on what I had already decided since the last time I was there—and every time before.

"One char kway teow please, medium size, extra cockles."

I pulled out my wallet and took out the dollars that had been waiting so long to be spent. As I unfolded them, Grandma appeared, seemingly out of nowhere, offering her food court discount card that she clutched in her hand. "Come, take—I pay." Short and to the point. No need for the frills of full sentences, just four words that communicated everything that she needed to.

"It's OK, Grandma, I've got dollars," came my reply.

"Tsst." She shook her head with a slight frown. "Cheaper! Less 10 percent!"

My dollars would have to wait. Their time would come and they would probably end up in the pocket of the Ice Cream Sandwich uncle on Orchard Road. I knew better than to argue with Grandma over paying for food—this lesson I had learned before. Grandma handed over her card. I wonder whether the joy she gained from the transaction came more from buying her grandson a meal or from saving 10 per cent. I thanked her and she shuffled off to pay for another family member, her frailty seemingly dissipating with every purposeful step.

I sat down with my food. Other family members would inspect my plate and comment, "looks good!" in approval of both my choice and the quality of the food. Once the inspection and analysis was over, it was my time to enjoy my meal. Everything else faded as I carefully looked through my char kway teow, neatly sitting on a woody-beige palm leaf on my plate. Each ingredient, carefully folded together to create harmony. This dish represents the Singapore that I love and hold dear to my heart: the unity of two different types of noodles—kway teow and yellow egg noodles, both sharing the limelight and also humbly creating a platform upon which the other ingredients can shine. To me, this dish reflects the harmony across cultures and the selflessness Singaporeans show: the sambal chilli providing flavour, heat and beads of sweat with each mouthful, just like the tropical climate; the cockles serving as a reminder of the ever-present sea and the origins of the fishing villages that gave Singapore its name, *Temasek,* or "Sea Town"; further emphasised by the thinly sliced Chinese sausages that curl into long boats like the sampans of yesteryear. Lastly, the invisible ingredient that pulls the whole dish together: wok hei. This is the dark, smoky flavour that comes from cooking in a wok over a very hot flame—it cannot be "added", yet it is ever-present. I see this in Singapore, too.

There is an undefinable flavour to Singapore—I'm not sure what it is, but I love it.

The cacophony of family catching up and discussing food suddenly brought me back into the busy kopitiam. Holding onto my wife's arm, Grandma was last to sit down, ready to tuck into her mee pok, victorious in her loyalty card savings for the day. As we ate, talked and laughed, I had a sense of excitement for more time in my country of birth. Little did I know that in time to come, I would be making that same journey with a one way ticket, my family and I returning home for good.

***

Food plays such a huge part in my memories, nostalgia and sense of home in Singapore. My visits back to Singapore as a child were filled with hawker visits and family get-togethers. Every trip back we would have a big family reunion, where all the aunties would bring their own dish to share with everyone. This sort of mass feeding is very popular in Singapore, even with the younger generations. Either we were very lucky in our "potluck" meals, or someone was organising it all behind the scenes. The food was always delicious and I would do my best to try everything. The food was never there just for sustenance—it was a talking point and my mother and her sisters would discuss recipes and how they made everything. I have a vague memory of one of these occasions at my Uncle Robin and Auntie Lorraine's house. It was night-time and I could hear the cicadas. The older cousins were skipping around the swimming pool, singing, "Here we go round the mulberry bush." I remember wanting to join in, but I felt I couldn't. I'm not sure why, perhaps it was my age, perhaps it was my unfamiliarity, being abroad.

As an adult, I still sometimes felt a distance or unfamiliarity with my cousins. They always treated me like family, looking out for me, staying in touch despite the long distance and time difference, but I missed out on a lot of time together. They made heaps of memories with each other as kids, building their friendships. They had in-jokes and common experiences and so I am slowly playing catch up. My cousins and I are a bit of a clan—there are 21 of us altogether, all on my mother's side. In my childhood years I would hear lots about Elliot and I would be most interested in him. There were a few photos of us together and so there was a greater connection to him than any others. Li-ann and E-yen came to live in the UK in their late teens, and so we got to know them a little more too. I used to be scared of E-yen. Into my later teens I spent more time with Shaun and Jeremy. They took me out to nightclubs and we finished those nights with breakfast or chicken rice at 4am—more food experiences interlacing my relationship with Singapore.

***

Jeremy is a well-respected chef in Singapore. Actually, he is so much more than that but for the purpose of this chapter, this is the side of his character upon which I'd like to focus. His talents in the kitchen and his drive as an entrepreneur have seen him establish some wonderful food businesses in Singapore. He is passionate about local food and is considered a curator of the best hawker foods. Recently, Jeremy showcased a number of hawkers at the top of Singapore's most iconic hotel, Marina Bay Sands, giving these local chefs a platform and status they truly deserve. The best roasted belly pork I have ever eaten was one that Jeremy made. It was at one of those huge family reunions— Christmas 2015. Our daughter, Aspen, was just six months old and my parents were living in Singapore at the time. They hired a huge conference room in order to be able to fit everyone in. By this time, Jeremy's reputation as a top chef was already founded and so there was great anticipation around what he would bring to the potluck dinner. Usually, at this sort of occasion, I am very good at taking a small amount of everything, leaving enough for others to try a fair share of all that is on offer. However, I am sure I hogged the pork—no pun intended.

I wanted to discover a little more about my heritage and, with the food culture in Singapore being so prominent, I felt that exploring heritage food may be a good way to gain an even better understanding. Of course, I decided that Jeremy would be a great person to ask. While we were still living in the UK, he presented a short TV show that caught my attention and has remained in my mind until now. He had found some photos of days gone by and was researching the heritage and the stories behind those photos. In the programme, he met a lady who used to sell nasi lemak as a child, and her story intrigued me as her childhood seemed so Victorian. I loved the way Jeremy so comfortably got involved with the lady, chanting, "Naaaasi lemak! Nasi lemaaaak!"

I didn't really know what to expect after I told Jeremy I wanted to discover some heritage food, but I felt like I had so much to learn, and that whatever I experienced was going to be insightful. He asked me to meet him at Golden Mile Food Centre. I was excited about this as Millie had been a few times and it is known as one of Singapore's more iconic and older hawker centres. I took the MRT one Sunday afternoon and strolled a five minute walk from the station to the hawker centre. I walked up the stairs and was greeted with an overwhelming number of food stalls. There must have been well over a hundred, each serving their own specialty—recipes that have been cooked and tweaked and cooked and tweaked some more until they reached absolute perfection. It was so nice to see people out and about, filling chairs and eating together—still separated into pairs (because of the COVID-19 regulations at the time), but going about their lives. Since relocating to Singapore we had not yet experienced a non-pandemic life. I met Jeremy, who was already tucking into a plate of hokkien mee. To my delight, he had a pair of chopsticks waiting for me and I had the chance to tuck into the food with him. This was not part of the food discovery afternoon, but just Jeremy's lunch!

When chatting with Jeremy, I realised how much he looked like my Kong Kong in the black-and-white picture on my mother's dressing table. High cheekbones, slim face, jet black hair. Jeremy explained that he was excited about the afternoon as this was one of the best places to come for good food. He also explained that Golden Mile was considered an "Army Market"—somewhere that lads, while serving National Service, would come to top up on their supplies: boot polish, bags and all-sorts were available on the floor above us. I loved this sort of information, a bit of insight into the Singaporean life I had not lead, but could have led—experiences that I did not gain myself, but could imagine through the stories and experiences of others.

I followed him as he took off. Like a creature in its natural habitat, Jeremy sniffed around and moved confidently through rows of food stalls, scanning each vendor and their produce. He described them as we went along, giving me back stories and successes. He would pause and continue every now and again, like a meerkat on alert—something had caught his attention, but then he carried on with his exploration. We passed one very interesting-looking hawker, who sold what appeared to be prawns that had been glued to a donut. Jeremy explained that COVID-19 had forced these chefs and entrepreneurs to find a new outlet, as they would normally have been selling their food at big events—weddings, parties and other corporate meetings. They took a risk and opened a hawker stall, and there, I could see the proof of their delicious food—a long line, full of people waiting for their lunch!

Eventually we stopped at an unassuming stall. There was a big red sign that read "Charlie's Peranakan Food". Charlie had been a very successful chef and decided to retire some years ago. After eight years of being out of the game, and after many people had called for Charlie to come back, he had reopened his stall and Jeremy said it was among the best Peranakan food available across the whole country. Out front of Charlie's stall was a white drywipe board with Charlie's menu, listed in different colours. No frills, no big printed menus, no neon lights. Hand-written, some rubbed out and some replaced. The alternating blue, red and black colours was the only creativity that went into the design of the menu board—possibly the colours that came in the packet. Simply done, the old way. I gazed down, scouring the dishes on offer for something I recognised. There were many unfamiliar names. Even some combinations of letters I wasn't sure how to pronounce. I suddenly felt like a foreigner.

A few dishes stood out to me as familiar—beef rendang, ngoh hiang... mutton rendang counts as another dish, right? I saw chap chye—a dish I knew the name of, but I had no idea what it was. Over the years of returning to Singapore, my aunties would cook all these wonderful dishes and I would eat them all, but I had no idea what they were called. Jeremy ordered, I watched, feeling a little more like an outsider when I struggled to understand the Singlish phrases and accents, beneath the distortion of the big fans blowing to keep patrons cool. Jeremy moved some food crates off from the table he wanted to sit at—a small action that highlighted his comfort and confidence in this environment. Forever feeling the tension of being an immigrant in my own country, it also highlighted to me that I was not as comfortable or confident in this setting as I thought I was.

The food soon arrived while Jeremy was off buying drinks and I felt a wave of relief when I could see dishes that I recognised. My comfort levels and confidence returned.

"This vegetable dish is super familiar—what is it called?" I asked Jeremy. I could imagine the taste just by looking at it.

"This one is chap chye," he replied, surprised I didn't know its name.

"Oh! Before this point, I knew the name, chap chye, and I knew this dish, but I have never put them together as the same thing!" This was my problem: having only been here for big family get-togethers, I knew the flavour of dishes—I ate them all! But I didn't know what any of them were called. As kids and cousins, we would only ever grab our food and then go and play together—the parents would have all been catching up having been apart for a few years, and so we wouldn't often have a grown-up telling us what these dishes were. After all, my cousins all grew up eating these foods—they didn't need to ask! Strangely, I have definitely heard my older sister talking about chap chye, but I had not ever felt the need to ask her what she was referring to.

The next dish was babi hong, a very familiar looking dish. One of my favourite meals growing up was lor bak—a braised pork belly dish in dark soy sauce and five spice. Jeremy explained that this was very similar, but had been put together using a rempah. Another word I had heard but didn't know the meaning to—this was a big afternoon of discovery for me! Rempah is the Malay word for spice, but it is used as a term for a paste made of shallots and garlic and used as the base of a dish. The flavours of this were like childhood to me. Like Remy in the Disney film *Ratatouille*, I had sparks of colour appear in my mind as I ate. Jeremy described the rempah being made by Nyonyas in days gone by, using their pestle and mortar, or *batu lesung* to break down the shallots and garlic, adding chillies and other spices, depending on the dish they were creating. When we visited The Intan a few months previously, Baba Alvin had

One of my favourite places in Singapore—the top of Puaka Hill on Pulau Ubin.

Family Pot Luck at an auntie's home in 2014.

A family reunion, Christmas 2015.

My packlist for the pilgrimage—I didn't realise how heavy it would all be!

Four generations of Tan men, in 2020.

Aspen, our little *nyonya*. I wonder which parts of her heritage she will embrace as she grows up.

Sarong kebayas and batik shirts, celebrating the Lunar New Year 2021.

Milo and Aspen—Singapore is their playground.

My favourite *char kway teow.*

We will always celebrate National Day (2021) in red!

Today's kids playing with the statues of the children of times gone by.

Milo playing chess with my grandpa—I am so grateful they have this special time together.

On our round island cycling tour, the children completed 182km in 5 days.

mentioned that there was so much skill in the use of the *batu lesung* that matchmakers would see a lady as more suitable if she could use it well. That gives a whole new meaning to the phrase "You crushed it!"

We worked our way through a delicious beef rendang and Jeremy explained the differences between the Peranakan rendang and the Indonesian one—the latter being more creamy with more sauce. The flavour was smooth and coconutty, and my taste buds approved of my ancestors' recipes. The ngoh hiang was delicious, with generous chunks of prawn and fatty pieces of pork wrapped in a crispy skin. I added the sambal belachan that was neatly resting in a small dish—a chilly sauce that perfectly complemented the food.

Lastly, we came onto the buah keluak. This is a typically Peranakan dish: a big, golf ball-sized seed, sometimes referred to as the black nut. The nut itself takes days of preparation, as it naturally contains cyanide—a deadly poison. Its name, buah keluak, literally means "the fruit which nauseates", and it takes up to five days of soaking and ten water changes to draw all of the poison out. Chef Charlie had prepared it by taking out the inside of the nut after soaking and then cooking it with a personalized rempah that accentuate the nut's flavour, before spooning it all back into the nut shells and then cooking with the meat (in this case, pork ribs, but sometimes chicken wings). It was served with a popsicle stick for digging out the black paste from the inside of the shell. It looked like it could be grainy, but its texture was smooth on the palette. The buah keluak had a very strong flavour, perhaps a little musty, like a strong mushroom. I recognised the flavour, but I couldn't place where I had tasted it before. I definitely didn't remember ever eating a buah keluak before. It turns out I recognised the flavour from Jeremy's own sambal, from his spice paste company, The Batu Lesung Spice Company.

As we left Charlie's, I asked Jeremy about the future of good Peranakan food. If Charlie's is really among the best and the food is rarely that good, where do we access good heritage food when Charlie decides to hang up his apron for good? Jeremy struggled to answer the question, and I don't blame him. Perhaps there isn't a current solution to this problem. In this day and age of social media, food that is largely brown in colour, accompanied by rice and served in a hawker centre doesn't have the Instagram-appeal as a deep pink slice of salmon resting on some golden couscous, garnished with a rich green salad, served in a boujee restaurant. Is quality Peranakan food and its future solely reliant on the likes of Violet Oon and her high-end set-ups? I hope not, but the quality of food we had at Charlie's can only come from a passion that is hard to replicate.

***

We wrapped up lunch with a dessert of glutinous rice balls which were filled with peanuts (in a ginger soup) and black sesame (in a peanut soup). Jeremy had planned to show me how to cook something that he hoped would spark my memories, but first we needed to go and buy some ingredients. We had spent such a long time enjoying (a little too much) food, that the wet market was closed, but Jeremy knew of a

Thai supermarket nearby that would sell some quality fresh produce, so we took a walk.

There is a block of apartments along Beach Road that offers a wide view across the Kallang River to Singapore's National Stadium, and all the way to the glass domes of the Gardens By The Bay and the Supertrees. This retro-vintage looking block may not be as iconic as Marina Bay Sands or other giants of the Singapore skyline, but it belongs nonetheless. It boasts bright yellow lines and circles that don their own personality. It is underneath these apartments where the Thai supermarket sits. The retro vintage vibe is not exclusively from its exterior, as the inside feels a little dated, too—brown-tiled flooring and open pipes made me feel like I had gone back in time. But it wasn't without its charm. Jeremy explained that the lease on this particular building of apartments and shops was up in about 20 years, and that it was very likely that it would be demolished to make way for another super-modern block. I couldn't help but feel that this relentless modernisation will also stop us from being able to see and understand our own origin story. Like the food at Charlie's making way for high-end restaurants, fusion cuisine and insta-worthy presentation. I love creativity and recognise that for creativity to flourish, often the old needs to be modernised or, at worst, left behind—but I hope amidst this tension we are able to keep our heritage food, stories and some traditions.

***

We made our way back to Jeremy's home in a taxi and it was nice to be able to sit and take in the surroundings. Often, in

Singapore, I travel by MRT, the underground network of trains. It has its positives, but my geography of over-ground is not so good! Sometimes, I'll look at a map and I am always surprised at how close certain places are. Once, sitting at the top of the Pan Pacific hotel, Millie and I were amazed to see that City Hall, Bugis, Chinatown and the Arab Quarter were all so close to each other. We were even able to look out over the whole island and see Malaysia in the distance!

A passionate chef, Jeremy's kitchen is beautiful. It is spacious with room to move and I was looking forward to what he was going to prepare for me, and what I was going to learn. He decided to show me how to cook a very simple vegetable curry, sayur lodeh. This is a dish that I immediately associate with our family reunions and the food we all shared. I honestly had no idea how easy it was to make and our process was made even easier by using one of Jeremy's *batu lesung* pastes. It sat in the pan, cooking complete. Just the image of the cabbage, carrots and green beans in a yellow curry sauce brought me back. I took a spoonful and chewed.

"The vegetables are a bit harder than I remember them," I shared with Jeremy. The sayur lodeh I remembered was much softer, like it had been cooked longer.

"Of course," Jeremy replied, "the one we have at our family parties has been cooked forever by one of the aunties, then brought to someone's house and then heated up again! It's actually more authentic when it is softer!"

A good point. The more I thought about it, the experience of this dish created something more authentic in the making.

Cooked by one of our mothers, probably while trying to organise their kids to get ready to go to the family reunion, bringing it to an auntie's house, reheating it, and sharing it with the family. That's real, authentic heritage food.

I loved spending time with Jeremy that day, exploring the hawker centre, chatting about past family reunions and learning about heritage food. I was surprised how little I knew about the food I was eating. I had no idea there was an Indonesian rendang and a Peranakan rendang. I didn't know about the buah keluak and the complexities around making it. I guess I was left wondering about the other Peranakans, like me or my children, who don't necessarily know the history and stories of their heritage. I have only been able to discover heritage food by looking for it and I am fortunate enough to have someone like Jeremy in my life who is happy to show me what he has only discovered through his own personal journey and passion for food. Hopefully this book goes a little toward raising that awareness. Perhaps it will help to ignite a curiosity and a journey of discovery for some other young Peranakans, who have been distanced from the lives of their forefathers and the foods that are so intertwined with their heritage.

***

There are many aspects to Singapore's food culture that go towards creating that sense of home for me. Firstly, it is so accessible—great food at an affordable price. We spent our first six weeks in Singapore waiting for our kitchen things to arrive in a container from the UK. We would explore our new local area and I had to resist buying new plates or bowls, so as not to overload our kitchen once everything arrived. I had also just bought a set of plates and bowls from Le Creuset in the UK. I love cooking and I have a fairly unhealthy obsession with the Le Creuset range! So we spent the best part of six weeks eating out at hawker centres, food courts and coffee shops. Coffee shops in Singapore have a very different vibe to the coffee shops in the UK. In the UK, coffee shops were exactly that: shops that sell coffee, as well as tea, other drinks and sometimes cakes and pastries—basically cafés… but not to be mistaken with a cafe (pronounced "kaff"). A cafe, on the other hand, is a greasy diner, where you can get a full English breakfast for under a tenner. They serve tea in chunky mugs and the portions are usually enormous. In Singapore, coffee shops are like smaller hawker centres with fewer stalls. They are still open air, with fans circulating a breeze instead of aircon and are part of a building, rather than free-standing stalls.

This easy-access food culture builds community. Interactions are friendly. Cultures are blended. Chinese food stalls sit next to Indian food stalls, which sit next to Malay food stalls, next to western food stalls, next to Indonesian, next to Japanese, next to Korean, next to fusion and more! Families eat food from other cultural backgrounds to their own, tasting the flavours of different heritages. Another way community is built and society is taught, is in the active trust that takes place in every hawker and food court—you can reserve your table with just a packet of tissues. Place a packet of tissues on a table and people will assume it is taken by someone in an act referred to as *chope*. Others may *chope* their table with a bag, knowing it will not be stolen. I even saw an iPhone placed on a table to reserve it—no one even considered taking it (the phone or the table!). These little interactions to me are a microcosm of Singapore's wider culture.

Recent news stories and reports from the UK, Australia and America of abductions and missing children have given me a fresh appreciation of Singapore's safety. I was overwhelmed with tears when a four-year-old Australian girl, Cleo Smith, was found by authorities. She had been kidnapped from the same tent in which her parents were sleeping and was missing for 18 days. Here in Singapore, we take for granted that our kids can be handed some money and sent off for a wander around a hawker centre, before returning with their drink of choice as well as the correct change. I don't know if I'd have the confidence to do the same thing in the UK.

***

The cross-section of society, seen in the wide and varied foods and dishes, is complimented by the cross-section of history that can be tasted in each dish. Even Singapore's national dish, chilli crab, is an amalgamation of geographical and historical contexts. Crab, from the seas around this island, mixed with chilli, a spice of the region, combined with a modern and tangy condiment, left over by the British colonialists—tomato ketchup, eaten with bread—perhaps surprisingly, not rice. I love that food from different areas of the world can *belong* in Singapore. None of it is considered "foreign", it's all local. It reminds me that we are all immigrants, but all local, too. Malay, Chinese, Indian and western foods are all standards at hawker centres and it's all very good and authentic. I remember five years ago trying some western food at a hawker centre and thinking it was terrible—but these days the standard is great.

We all have our favourites in the hawker centres. Aspen loves chicken porridge (made from rice—very different to the oaty version we get in the UK), Milo's favourite is roast pork rice, Millie has become a nasi lemak connoisseur and I will forever be drawn to a smoky char kway teow. But despite having our favourite go-tos, we continue to explore the different foods on offer. Millie has become the most adventurous eater, enjoying everything from laksa to chendol, from rendang to durian. Every now and again she will make a point to make her way around every stall in a food court—not all in one go, of course! Whenever we try something new we will aim to have it from two different stalls to see which we prefer, trying to refine our taste buds. Many conversations and friendship bonds are created around food, discussing the best version of a particular dish, where to get it and what makes it so good. I feel like I am fast becoming Singaporean to this extent and even find myself queuing up for food at a stall I have not yet tried, just because there is a long queue!

Sometimes our children's memories are triggered by the food they have eaten. They remember the first durian ice kachang they tried—we were with a friend who had never had durian before and the kids always talk about that experience when they have ice kachang. I once had an amazing lamb shank biryani after paddleboarding to Marina Bay from East Coast Park, and now every biryani sends me back to that day. I love how food can connect us through time and space. Sayur lodeh does that for me too: it sends me to family gatherings. But even more significantly other dishes connect us to our ancestry and origins. One of my favourite things to eat in Singapore is cincalok—a fermented shrimp sauce. It is salty, fishy and sharp: a sauce that dates back to the Portuguese settlers in Melaka in the 1500s. We usually have it with steamed pork belly, and the fermented shrimp is fried up with shallots, chilli and topped off with a squeeze of lime. It's a dish that brings me back to my childhood—it was one of my father's favourite things to eat when we were kids, and I love that there is a connection to not just that time and memory, but all the way back through history to a time where there were no freezers or refrigerators and so things had to be salted and fermented to make them last.

Food is a true Singaporean passion. I don't mean that eating is a Singaporean pastime, nor do I mean that cooking is a Singaporean pastime. "Food" becomes a category of its own, that only really makes sense here. Food culture is something that, to me, has helped to create Singapore's identity. After all, Singapore hawker culture has been added to the UNESCO Representative List of Intangible Cultural Heritage of Humanity. This award just helps to give gravitas to something that we already knew: Singapore food culture is a very special thing. I am proud of it, proud to be a part of it and proud to share it with my friends when they come to visit.

Chapter 12

Home

We all have a good idea of what it is to feel at home: comfortable, relaxed, at peace. We furnish our homes with the things we love and value. Comfy cushions, pictures of loved ones, furniture that is designed in a way that we enjoy the look of. We paint our homes colours that make us feel relaxed, we have ornaments that remind us of something, or represent something special to us. Artwork represents us. We feel comfortable to be messy at home. Our bedrooms are where we hide away, where we rest, where we are intimate, where we make our daily transitions from unpresentable to presentable! We invite people into our homes, letting them into a piece of ourselves, opening the front door to vulnerability. When we invite our friends over, we are always at risk of showing people what our family is *really* like, mainly because children are unpredictable and we may have to do some real parenting in front of our friends!

A few years before I met Millie and got married, I was living in a terraced house with Owen and Phil, who I have mentioned a few times in this book. We unfortunately had a reputation of not having the tidiest of homes and one Sunday our Pastor asked us to help look after a special guest preacher called Nick Caine.

Nick and his wife, Christine, run an incredible charity in Europe called A21, where they are instrumental in combatting human trafficking as well as providing rehabilitation and ongoing support for those rescued from the sex trade. We had not anticipated having to host him at our home and so, as normal, our house wasn't really ready for any guests. Owen was driving and Nick was in the front when Nick asked whether there was anywhere he could use a bathroom. To our embarrassment and mild panic, Owen's only thought was that he could use our place. Nick entered through the front door, which led directly into my bedroom. To this day, I still claim that my room was normally tidier than the boys' rooms, so this was probably OK. Nick then had to navigate our living room and kitchen before reaching the bathroom, at the back of the house.

He came back out of the front door, closed it behind him and made his way to the car. We were a bit embarrassed about what he would have seen—the thought that we had just opened our messy home to an honoured guest. He sat down in the front passenger seat, closed the door and there was an awkward silence... "There's a roll of gaffa tape on your toilet," he said, with a slight grin at the strange find. "Everything about you says something about you!" We didn't know how to respond, so we just looked back at him, our slight grin brought on by embarrassment.

I have no idea what that roll of tape was doing in our bathroom, nor what it said about us! Our homes are intimate places where we can totally be ourselves—even if that means messy—in the physical or emotional.

***

We know *with whom* we can feel at home, too. For some guests to our home we feel the need to roll out the red carpet, take out fancy snacks and serve wine, to make a good first impression. Other visitors are like family, where we don't need to put up a front. To be clear: the front we put up when hosting unfamiliar visitors is still genuine, but more polished. Our more familiar friends, hopefully, will know they are valued already. We are blessed in having a fair few of those comfortable friends in Singapore. I feel I am still missing the deeper friendships—friendships that take years to build—but we haven't lived here all that long and it takes time to make those friendships. Despite this, for me Singapore has that feeling of comfort. Singapore has a feeling similar to a living room full of familiar friends—the people, the culture, the way of life.

It is worth mentioning my faith here and how that has given me a strong sense of life purpose. Singapore provides freedom to maintain a faith, too. England is seen as a Christian country, particularly with the Anglican church being tied to the country and its history. However, the pathway of religion is scattered with eggshells and it is hard to hold beliefs that are different to anyone else's. Individuality is watered down to protect uniqueness. Holding a strong belief or value is often seen as narrow-minded and anti everyone-who-doesn't-believe-the-same-as-you. Christmas lights in high streets are now referred to as "illuminations" and Easter is all about chocolate.

In Singapore I see a true embrace of all religions. To hold strong values is respected and cherished, and there is unity in the blend of religions: a focus on what you *do* believe in, rather than what you *do not* believe in. You can walk around the Arab Street area and hear the call to prayer every day. Every Christmas, the famous Tangs department store on Orchard Road displays a Bible verse as part of their festive displays. There are always displays of religion, tradition and faith at different times of the year and they are respected by the populace. As someone with a strong faith, this contributes to my sense of home.

***

The atmosphere changes when it rains in Singapore. There's a humidity and a cool—a damp yet fresh smell. It is hard to describe why, but it makes me feel at home. I also experience that scent and warmth on some evenings. Millie and I will often watch a show on the television at the end of the evening before we go to bed. We love outdoor adventure shows and nature shows, too. We have pretty little water fountains outside our balcony and I love the sound of running water, but we usually close the balcony doors and turn on the air-conditioning in the evenings so that we can hear our programs! Millie's bedtime routine is far more complex than mine, which usually involves brushing my teeth and climbing into bed, and so I spend a few moments on the balcony alone. I love the contrast of stepping out of the cool air-conditioned room into the warmth and haze of a Singapore night-time. It takes me back to one of my parents' friend's house—I'm not sure why, but it was a happy memory. As I stand out on the balcony, I breathe in the Singapore air and I feel grateful to be here.

I remember when my grandparents would open their suitcases after returning from Singapore. They would usually have some treats inside: jars of kaya, the local coconut jam, and bakkwa, a sweet barbecued pork. I often refer to it as Singapore's answer to biltong. As they opened their suitcases, there was a split second when I could just smell the tropical air of Singapore.

In July 2020, relocating to Singapore, we were put under a 14 day quarantine. It was a most welcome break and a forced rest, which we needed more than we realised. We were assigned an iconic hotel—the Mandarin Oriental in Marina Bay, and were given a suite to enjoy. We had a beautiful view, looking over the Pan Pacific hotel and the towers at South Beach. The one thing we did not have was fresh air. The room had a glass door, which was understandably locked as there was no longer a balcony— just a 13 storey drop—but on leaning against it one afternoon in our second week, I realised that a tiny gap would appear and I could hear the outside world and smell that wonderful tropical air. The prolonged journey of getting to Singapore and the stress of arriving during COVID made that brief sniff of fresh air only add to my feeling of yearning for Singapore—and it made the completion of our quarantine and those first steps of residency in my country of birth all the more liberating.

***

Throughout my life I have been blessed with security, love and care. I have become more aware of this as I have gotten older, but time and experience does that. It shows you a wider scope of life and teaches you to be grateful for what you have. One evening

I was having a chat with a friend. He and his wife were yet to have children and he was expressing his thoughts and concerns about himself as a father. I remember telling him that as long as he was present and showed love, his kids would be fine. Over my teaching career of 13 years now, I can confidently say that regardless of background or financial status, the most balanced children come out of a loving family. Love in its unconditional form helps to develop a sense of security. Receiving this from my parents showed me that whenever I mess up, whenever I got things drastically wrong, whenever I was rude or unkind or distant, that they would always love me, no matter what. One of the things that has driven me to find conclusions in this journey is that I know I had it good—life hasn't been without its challenges, but I have had it good. Yet, I found home away from where I grew up. I found home, physically, away from my family.

While I continue to process my thoughts, feelings and the journey I have been on so far, I wonder whether I have actually found home in my parents, despite finding it 8,000 miles (12,800 kilometres) away from them. It was they who placed the Singaporean culture in our childhood home, they who gave me an amazing example of family, they who showed me what it was to be safe and secure. They were the ones who created the memories on holidays, who brought us to our family reunions— they were the ones who brought a helper into our home and taught her how to look after their son. Perhaps this apple didn't fall too far from the tree.

We regularly try to teach our own children about the wonderful aspects of Singapore. I worry sometimes as a parent, whether the foundations we lay will be strong enough, whether they will be drawn to safety and security. This journey has forced me to really consider the things that influenced me as a child—all of the love, but also the trauma and abuse, too. While these are at the forefront of my mind I have thought intensely about how to protect our children, and how to draw the balance of protecting their innocence while allowing them to grow independent and strong. I have to remind myself that the love my parents gave us helped me to navigate the storms of life and that the same will be true for my own children as we continue to love them and do our best.

***

Throughout this journey I have often wondered why my internal homing beacon wasn't activated until that trip in 2014. I was 29 years old by then and had returned to Singapore six or seven times. Perhaps it was adulthood and an awareness of self that hadn't matured until then. Perhaps it was the seemingly fast approach of my 30s. I really struggled turning 30. I'm not sure why, I just didn't feel ready to let go of my 20s. Actually, come to think of it, I'm still not ready to let go of my 20s! I guess a lot had changed since my previous visit to Singapore. It had been my longest stretch without coming back. In my last visit, I was 23 and single, still young and enjoying the nightlife scene. Six years on and I had gained not just a wife and child, but an appreciation for culture and heritage. My idea of relaxation was no longer sitting on a beach for two weeks, but to immerse myself in a place, in the people of the country.

This change in mindset had been particularly noticeable on a big family holiday in France in 2012. My parents had organised a fantastic two-week break for all of us—my parents, my older sister and family, my younger sister and her husband, and Millie and me. We had a day to spend in the beautiful city of Bordeaux and after a coffee and croissant together in the morning, we all split off into our little subsections of family. When we re-gathered in the evening, Millie and I had scoured every last corner of the city, its river, architecture and history, getting into a few museums and eating plenty of cheese, too!

Perhaps this new habit of discovering places and understanding the people of those places encouraged me to want to understand Singaporeans and thus myself. Millie and I had made a little pact that we would not return to a holiday destination as there was so much of the world to see. For our fifth wedding anniversary we went to Venice for a few nights. I remember standing on the Rialto Bridge on our last afternoon before taking the water taxi to the airport, looking out over the Grand Canal and trying to take in every sight I could, knowing that it was unlikely we'd ever return. It seems sad, yet there is so much out there that I have yet to experience. I only just learned about Hang Son Doong—a giant cave in Vietnam, discovered in 2009, that is so large that a Boeing 747 can comfortably fly through, and a 40-storey skyscraper can fit inside. I've yet to go there but it has been added to my ever-growing bucket list.

We felt the same way about Singapore. In 2014, we thought it was a once in a lifetime visit—maybe once in a decade, as we had family connections. So we lined up every tourist thing you can think of to fill our five week holiday, assuming we wouldn't do it again. What followed was five weeks of intense learning about Singapore—full emersion into the life, people, food, tourist attractions and landmarks of this tiny yet jam-packed nation. And we loved every second of it and every square metre of the place. The National Day Parade was a highlight for me. We watched it on the television at my parents' apartment and it struck me how Singapore honoured every aspect of society—not just a parade to demonstrate military prowess. I watched, proud of my roots, as shop workers and office workers paraded, displaying the flags of their companies and honouring them for playing their part in the success of the nation. Perhaps the theme of that 2014 parade, "Our People, Our Home", impacted me more than I knew at the time.

***

As I have explored my own journey and, at times, used it as a case study to understand others like myself, I have often looked ahead to the future, when my own children may ask their own questions of heart, heritage and home. Millie and I have made the decision that Singapore will be their home, the place they will grow up and make friends and memories. It is the culture in which we have chosen for our children to be immersed and the culture we want them to adopt. In time, we will explore permanent residency and even citizenship and along with this comes the decision that, unlike me, Milo will have the opportunity to serve Singapore in National Service. I hope he will take the opportunity with pride and dedication. Most encouragingly for us, they will grow up safe, with a freedom and innocence that is rare in the world today. I hope they will adhere to Singapore's rules and see them as safety rather than control. I hope they grow up to understand the value of these rules. I do occasionally wonder whether Singapore is too strict, too controlling, but in weighing up the alternatives, for us as a family, this is an option we had the luxury to choose, and it is the option we have chosen—to live in Singapore and to live by its laws.

As our children grow up in Singapore and develop a life with local friends and family, I wonder whether they will miss the UK. They do miss family. Currently we are only connected through screens—video calling a significant blessing in this period of global disconnection. I know that when the skies reopen, our friends and family will be much closer again. I wonder whether they will ever tire of the heat, ever miss the changing seasons. I wonder whether they will take for granted the convenience of Singapore. I'm not sure about any of the answers to this. Perhaps in the years to come they will visit the UK and wonder why they feel so connected. That will be their journey to travel, but for now I am loving seeing them make memories here in Singapore. I feel grateful that they can become familiar with certain places—the park connectors, the zoos, the beaches, the hawkers and more. Watching them develop their own love for my country and make their own connections to it is special.

I am forever amazed and filled with gratitude that Millie and I were united on our decision to move to Singapore, but also in our love for the country and its culture. She, too, is discovering it really for the first time as her own nation and has her own stories to tell. I wondered whether, as I felt like a foreigner in the UK with my physical appearance being very eastern, that she felt like a foreigner in Singapore, with her physical attributes being very western. Interestingly, Millie doesn't feel foreign here. She feels the same belonging as I do. Occasionally, she will notice how a market stall owner will offer her strawberries and blueberries, but the moment she asks for longans and mangosteens, all seems to be right again.

***

As a "Third Culture Kid" growing up in the UK, I wasn't aware of the rich heritage I had in the 20th smallest country in the world. Into my teens and 20s, I would have said I knew myself really well, but I have really enjoyed delving into my own story, to have a greater understanding of myself. I believe I know myself a little better now. It all started as a question—a realisation that I felt different somewhere else. A realisation that I felt more *me* in a different setting. I never knew I was misplaced until I had found home.

As I pushed off, paddling towards the horizon of discovery, I wanted to find out and understand more about my home, heritage and where my heart was. I hit waves of doubt—where I belonged, whether I was an authentic Singaporean and whether I would ever catch a Singlish accent! The winds pulled me in new directions—understanding myself from a psychiatric point of view, learning that my DNA was not as expected. I rediscovered familiar lands from years ago—reconnecting with my childhood helper and rebuilding a relationship with her, as well as reminiscing about times gone by with family reunions.

There is still so much to discover, more memories to be made, more food to eat, more places to visit and more stories to learn. Singapore's rich history and multi-cultural influences intertwine many hundreds of connections from all over the globe, each significant to Singapore's story. This is just *my* Singapore story and I am glad it's just the start. One thing I have learned is that none of us started here in Singapore. Our ancestors are a beautiful blend of nationalities from all around the globe: the Sumatrans, Chinese, Indians, Southeast Asians and Europeans, all adding flavour to the identity of the Singaporean. Perhaps that is what makes Singapore so special and what connects us all. We are all immigrants to this nation, yet we are also all local. Perhaps this is not just my story, but yours, too.

About the Author

British by passport and Singaporean by blood, school teacher Jonty Tan has a love for nature, the arts and people. In his spare time, he and his family love to explore the local and wider world in Singapore, finding the extraordinary wonder in their everyday lives, documenting and sharing their experiences with the world via their YouTube channel, Wonderlust.